Finucane & Me

Finucane & Me

My Life with Marian

John Clarke

Gill Books

With thanks to Kathleen Lambe, Margaret Scott and James Morrissey, whose help and encouragement made this book possible.

Gill Books
Hume Avenue
Park West
Dublin 12

www.gillbooks.ie

Gill Books is an imprint of M.H. Gill and Co.

978 07171 9550 3

Design and print origination by OK Graphic Design, Dublin
Edited by Emma Dunne
Proofread by Esther Ní Dhonnacha
Printed and bound in Great Britain by Clays Ltd, Elcograf S.p.A.
This book is typeset in 12/22 pt Sabon.

The paper used in this book comes from the wood pulp of sustainably managed forests.

A CIP catalogue record for this book is available from the British Library.

5 4 3 2 1

‘There are two types of people in this world;
the Givers and the Takers – make the call…’

Anon

‘Those who cannot remember the past
are condemned to repeat it’

George Santayana

Dearest Marian,

The world you and I knew before you died has changed immeasurably.

We didn't know it, of course, but Covid-19 was already creeping through humanity in our last few weeks together.

What followed – the cocooning, the absences, the denial of a hug – seems particularly surreal in light of your timing. All the rituals of death and mourning were scrambled and left many of us even further adrift. It made it harder to grieve, to find distractions, and so was all the more conducive to introspection.

My few broken words about us at your funeral made kind people curious about how I was faring without you.

'How are you?'

'I'm grand.'

'No, really – how are you?'

Our old friends Patrick Farrelly and Kate O'Callaghan talked me into making a documentary on grief and loss, and it seemed appropriate for me to do it for all those faithful companions of yours, your listeners throughout your broadcasting years, rather than leave it to commentators from the sidelines.

My stumbling attempts to define grief seemed to resonate with viewers, although my efforts sounded feeble and futile to me. You of all people knew about a depth of grief so visceral it defies description.

When I agreed to write this book about our time together, I thought I might focus on the joys, the travels, the companionship on the great adventure. I wanted to write about what brought us together, what kept us together, the pact of madness that drove us to explore the world and made it so exciting and interesting for us both.

But how do you write a story about a long life and complex humanity without talking about guilt, loss, challenges, tragedy and human flaws? How do you give it a meaning without some kind of philosophical framework?

I am conscious of the tendency to deify the dead and that includes you, my love. You were as flawed as any other human being, as you would be the first to acknowledge. As readers will discover, you were one of the most tolerant women on earth, but your privacy and certain aspects of our lives were sacrosanct. So while I will try to deal honestly with our lives together, I do that while guarding your and other loved ones' privacy as carefully as I can.

A major part of my problem in writing this book is that I cannot or do not think sequentially, which compounds the challenge for everyone around me. You would certainly have something tart to say about that.

You and I spent many hours wondering at our purpose on earth, musing on the randomness of life and death and choice. I see no sequence in life, only randomness, which may be partly responsible for what has landed me in trouble from time to time. I seek memories that seem meaningless to others; I look for order in places where there is none. It's what makes the journey exciting but also, alas, so predictable.

As well as struggling to find order and a timeline of some kind, the process of delving into 86 years of a rackety, restless life and trying to make sense of it involves a reckoning. It's been a painful process at times. And memory, as I also discovered in this process, is a terribly fickle friend for ageing and other reasons that will emerge.

You and I were a fairly disorganised, haphazard pair. Remembering dates and names has been a challenge, which won't surprise you at all. Incidents I breezily ascribed to the 1960s turn out to have happened in the 1970s – I think. Important family events I had assigned to the 1980s actually happened in the 1990s. Some highly diverting stories had to be abandoned when, on closer examination, they turned out to lack any internal coherence due to geographical or timeline conflicts – and that's being kind to myself.

We kept no aides-mémoires in the form of diaries and were careless with documents. The fact that you and I moved house at least half a dozen times meant many of the few documents we kept ended up decaying in a damp garage.

As for photographs ... well, people seem very surprised that in 40 years we never took a photograph. In these days of instant multiple pictures it seems like a bizarre anomaly. But why would we take photographs when we were so busy being there? We knew what we saw. That was enough.

The upshot of it all is that, in spite of exhaustive efforts, I remain an unreliable narrator – above all because your remarkable memory, my love, is lost to me.

You would have been the firm corrective on the margins, reminding me of details, taking issue with my interpretations and my philosophy, as I like to call it.

Sometimes I look back at old RTÉ footage and I remember the kitchen conferences before a show, an interview, a discussion. I view clips from an old and modern Ireland that you had a hand in transforming, scenes from Africa where we did a lot of crying – and laughing – with Friends in Ireland stalwarts and did some good along the way.

The answer to the kind people's questions about my life without you is that the earth continues to spin and so do I. I've moved on in the sense that I did not remain stranded in a cloud of mourning. But I never stop talking to you.

For a man of 86 with various ailments and a near lifetime of bad habits, my body has been surprisingly resilient, although I think it's catching up on me, finally. The COPD is noticeable now; I need more blood transfusions and seem to have more allergies. The cataracts seriously impinge on my reading. Since you left, I've had cancer treatment and heart problems.

I get tired more easily and I fight it, of course – you would expect no less.

As someone said, old age is not for wimps.

But I can tell you straight, my love. It was a wonderful, wonderful life.

John

Finucane & Me

ONE

The First Journey

The public saw only a sliver of the Marian iceberg. She was quite deliberate about that. But there are whole parts of her that even I didn't know. We were as close as any couple can be; we soldiered in all sorts of weird places and did all sorts of daft things.

'But do we really know each other?' I asked her one day.

'I don't think so,' she said.

Have you ever sat there looking at the person you've been sharing your life with for 40 years, sharing your grief, laughter, love, hate and everything else, and thought, *Who the fuck is this? How did I get here?*

*

What did I see first? A tall blonde woman in red trousers. Gabby. Laughing. Surprising. A rare sight coming down the steps of Stephenson Gibney & Associates, the brash young architectural partnership shaking up the capital city, when women made up just a handful of the profession.

She was on a year's placement from Bolton Street's School of Architecture. Arthur Gibney was her boss and my closest friend. It was around half past five on a sunny summer's evening, and he and I had arranged to have a drink in the Crookit Bawbee, where Mr Charlie Haughey featured among Gibney's regular drinking companions.

We said hello. 'Are you waiting for the quare fella?' she asked. I said yes, and we chatted about her views on the demolition of old city buildings, while also noting that she was doing her internship with a company profitably designing their replacements.

'So you're joining the enemy?'

'I want to learn how to be a good architect,' she said gravely.

Would she like a drink, I asked. We were all heading for the pub, as it happened, so she and I went ahead together and talked about books, which morphed into a heated debate about Hemingway and his book on bullfighting. A discussion ensued about blood sports, which was satisfactory for neither party, until we were joined by Arthur, with a crowd from the firm, and the drinks started.

At around eight o'clock she said she had to go. I offered to walk her to the door, then to the corner of Baggot Street, from where she went on about her business, wherever she was going.

Gibney asked if I liked her.

'She's a very interesting woman,' I said. Anyone who can argue about Hemingway is always interesting.

'She's very distant,' said Gibney. Which was exactly what I found interesting about her. She was reserved. A bit standoffish. Just ... different. Her exit from the pub was a pattern I would come to recognise on other occasions. She always seemed to have 'appointments'. I think she had her escape route built in before she went anywhere.

Gibney, myself and some others had a regular Friday lunch to which some ladies from his office were usually invited. I asked him if he would invite 'yer wan'. He rolled his eyes.

'I don't care if she's cold,' I said. 'I like her anyhow.'

So a couple of days later, Marian duly arrived down with three other women. Lunch started at half past twelve. By the time the food arrived, around two or three, there were half a dozen bottles on the table.

Marian? She laughed and kept laughing till the tears ran down her face. Nobody could figure out why she was laughing. She thought she had arrived at some kind of Mad Hatter's tea party. She had never seen such quantities of drink being consumed in the middle of the day nor heard anything like the nonsense that was being spouted.

Lunch finished up around five, whereupon Gibney, the master of ceremonies, would decree that it was time for liqueurs – sambuca (we didn't set fire to them – that was for tourists) or limoncello, perhaps.

This was followed by another decree – 'a proper drink in a proper pub' – whereupon we would proceed to a pub and drink two pints. Following those, Gibney would say that they were nice pints, but we must have a man's drink. This heralded the whiskey course. By now on the Friday routine, it would be around ten o'clock and it always seemed a bit premature to go home. The next stop would be a nightclub, where closing time was in the early hours.

Marian and I sat together at one end of a table at that first Friday lunch. We attempted to elevate the conversation to a slightly higher plane. Completely futile. Naturally we ended up in a nightclub – a terrible kip in Leeson Street.

By then I had learned a few things about her. I knew that she was 20 years old, that she had read every known book on God's earth and was a keen debater. But she also seemed quite innocent. Sheltered, convent educated, a daily

Mass-goer when she lived at home, raised through the sieve of devout Catholicism and respectability by a teacher and a garda with proper social consciences. Good people who lived good lives and earned their pensions, kept their noses clean and worked regular hours in the service of family, church and community.

I was her polar opposite. I had a wife and three young sons at home. And I was 14 years older than her. A hard-living, hard-drinking atheist of 34, wheeling and dealing in property and the rag trade. I'm not too sure what Marian made of me. But there was a torrent of chemistry between us.

After a couple of meetings, I realised she was the only person I ever wanted to see. We shared an insatiable curiosity about the wider world and how it worked. A diligent student debater and activist, she was far too busy studying, saving the planet and marching in protests against apartheid and the ruination of Georgian Dublin. Debating seemed to take up an inordinate amount of her time.

What she heard in me, I think, was an alternative voice. I accepted almost none of the tenets she had been brought up with. She was a voracious reader who routinely parked up her little Fiat Uno opposite Eason's on O'Connell Street every Saturday, bought a book and spent the afternoon reading it there in the car or on Howth Head. Her knowledge of American and Russian literature suggested it wasn't the *Sacred Heart Messenger* she was buying.

In her efforts to navigate a path through a stifling society, she possibly viewed me as her number-one specimen, someone who agreed with absolutely nothing she had heard or seen, someone from another world, a world that worked much more in the grey. That may have been the attraction. I don't know. We never analysed it because we didn't have to. Within a few weeks we had fallen in love.

*

It was easy enough to bump into one another discreetly. Gibney, being our social organiser, ordained a fitness regime for the group at one point and this involved tennis in Shankill, where my friend and mentor, Sam Sherling, had a farm. Marian and her friend would come out to join us and Sam would open a bottle of whiskey and we would all sit around discussing philosophy, Plato and the meaning of Zen, or so we liked to think. There was some tennis played, it's fair to say, and Sam was a very serious man in terms of the human comedy. He was also running a lucrative international scrap-metal business.

Thirty years older than me, he had been my mentor since I was 20. The Sherlings were no ordinary family. Fleeing the pogroms, Sam's father, a devout Ashkenazi Jew, walked from Russia to Cork and sold needles, thread and scissors door to door before setting up a scrap-metal business in the 1920s. It was a whole other world, one barely visible from Ireland unless you were prepared to look.

What did I learn from Sam Sherling? I'm not sure. Sam was a very negative man in many ways, and I could be negative too about life. But Sam was negative in that way that nothing really matters, everything changes, life is for living now because tomorrow we may all be dead or in a gas chamber or expelled in a pogrom. Finucane felt he was a dangerous mentor because he was an anarchist. It's true that he was more than a little odd. I seemed to spend a lot of my time with oddities. I liked them.

All this was an eye-opener for her. She was suddenly entangled in these frenetic encounters among people who appeared to be making money in all sorts of bizarre ways, people who were totally cynical about the system and how it operated, with a complete disregard for societal and religious norms.

We had a few things in common, she and I. We had been born in Dublin, our mothers were teachers and we were big readers. Otherwise, we might as well have landed from different galaxies.

*

Like most Dubliners then, we were only a degree or two removed from rural Ireland.

My only sibling, Elizabeth, and I were fashioned from more liberal material. Sheila, our mother, born in 1904, was raised in County Longford by a woman who rolled her own cigarettes – held with a hairpin – and was living a kind of anti-clerical feminism decades before it ever hit the mainstream. Granny Cosgrove reared five daughters and two sons on a farm in Dalystown, a townland a few miles from Granard where I often spent holidays. When Dublin's North Strand was bombed during the war, Sheila feared another attack, so we moved to Granny's for several months since Granard was considered to be an unlikely target.

I was only four or five and frightened by the big old creaky farmhouse so was really happy to be allowed to sleep with Granny. This came with conditions. Her alarm went off at six every morning. This was a house where electricity and running water were way in the future and the toilet was a 'long drop' in the orchard. So, Granny's day began by turning on her Tilley lamp, fuelled by methylated spirits, and stoking the ashes to boil water for the tea.

Then she would turn on the crackly radio – the kind run on old batteries that had to be taken the three miles to Granard every Friday to be charged – and tune it to the BBC.

The rule was that I got a cup of tea if I didn't talk.

It was 1940, the Second World War was raging, and on her bedroom wall was a vast map of Europe, made up of bits of maps of France and Germany and other places all stuck together. Cigarette in one hand and box of coloured pins in the other, she listened to the BBC news, with all the static, crackles and bangs, and moved little red pins on the map indicating new troop movements on the Russian or German battle fronts. I followed the war in silence and learned all sorts of army things while drinking my tea with Granny.

Granny Cosgrove was also a bookworm. All through the war, six books arrived every month from Foyles, the London booksellers. A war of a different kind was in permanent spate between her and the local canon, who strode about in a black cassock terrifying the poor citizens of Granard – every citizen except my granny.

'I suppose you're readin' them books still, Mrs Cosgrove,' he would thunder. 'How is your war going?'

'That's a halfwit, John,' she would answer loudly in my direction, gathering me and my sister around her long apron. She reared us to dissent. She and my mother were fiercely anti-clerical while managing to square it with observing the Catholic rituals.

Granny's husband was a farmer who had a hardware shop and a house in Granard town, and the children's townie playmates included Kitty Kiernan – much later to be known as Michael Collins's fiancée – whose family owned the hotel across the street. Grandad had never gone to school but had a keen respect for Granny's well-stocked mind. When she decreed that all their girls would go to university, he agreed, which was no small concession from a man in the 1920s. Granny kept her promise despite his early death.

Her children were as fearless as she was. By the 1930s, Sheila, my future mother, had a teaching job between three different schools in County Kildare and rode everywhere on her motorbike.

She and my father, Desmond Clarke, met in Spiddal in the Galway Gaeltacht, where they went to learn Irish in 1933 – a romantic national movement in those days, until it became organised and lost its charm for my mother and my father. Sheila continued to do all the driving. I never saw my father behind the wheel of a car.

Desmond was the kindest and gentlest of fathers to Elizabeth and me, which was surprising because he had a very dark childhood with a mother who was an idiot by Sheila's reckoning.

His mother was Marcella Shaw, born into a well-heeled Kilcullen family and a life of displaying her talents as a singer and a pianist at afternoon teas and soirées before marrying a dashing young barrister called John Clarke, my grandfather, from North Mayo – Parnell's right-hand fundraiser in America – and giving birth to Desmond and Leonard.

John died young from tuberculosis. His fundraising activities clearly hadn't enriched him personally, and certainly curtailed his practice, because he died penniless and Marcella was ill-equipped to earn a living. Her answer was to place the boys in the O'Brien Institute, a kind of home for the children of the genteel on the northside of Dublin and, like most of those institutions, a fairly savage and austere place. Then she took off to Belfast and became a nurse to victims of the First World War, while Desmond tried to look after Leonard in the orphanage, probably thinking it a temporary arrangement.

But when Marcella emerged from her war effort, she married a widower and acquired three stepsons, and somehow Desmond and Leonard never got back into the family home. I think my father suffered a lot of hardship and hurt in his early life, although his children would never have known.

Desmond was a prodigy. He left school at 16, wrote his first book at 17 and got a job in a solicitor's office in Molesworth Street at 18. When an opening came up for an assistant librarian in the Royal Dublin Society in 1925, he grabbed it because it placed him back among books. By the time he retired as chief librarian in 1974, he had played a major role in developing the new RDS library and become a dominant modernising force in the Library Association of Ireland. He had also produced a prodigious number of published short stories, as well as works as diverse as art biographies and a study of 18th-century agriculture, histories, bibliographies and reviews, and became secretary of Irish PEN, among other things.

Desmond adored the west of Ireland, with its little cosmopolitan colonies of artists and writers, and he loved exploring the history and the heritage of the people along the seaboard, writing stories about them long before Connemara was colonised by Dublin 4.

Desmond also became chairman of the Beekeepers' Association and found time to pester the *Irish Times* letters editor about matters like the destruction of woods in Mount Merrion.

Perhaps the most extraordinary thing about him was that, in spite of his own deep childhood scars and poor role models, he adored his two kids, even me. He tried very hard to give us a life and the kind of love that he had never experienced. Although it was an age when children were casually slapped, my father never slapped us, nor did my mother. He thought slapping a child was a terrible thing to do.

He and Sheila had a good marriage. There was a lot of reading and a lot of books in the house. Like her own mother, my mother was anti-clerical while observing the Catholic rituals. My father never indicated much attachment to religion.

The only time I really saw him angry was about the exclusion of Catholics from Trinity, where some extraordinary research was happening in the sciences, a subject that was close to his heart. He felt that Irish people were being excluded from all this by a cleric, specifically John Charles McQuaid.

St Conleth's on Clyde Road was the chosen school

for my secondary education. Though founded as 'an establishment for the sons of Catholic gentlemen', it felt like a fairly broad, liberal-minded place that encouraged free and open thinking – another lucky life choice I shared with Marian – even for this young rebel without a cause. But unlike Marian, I was very hard work.

Coming of age in the 1950s, my problem was that there was nothing I liked about Ireland. I didn't like the Church, I didn't like the singularity of thought, I didn't like the social structures. Worse, when I was about 15, I started reading the existentialists and deciding this was the way to go. Life has no meaning, nothing happens, nothing matters, reject bourgeois conventions, whatever I do I will die one day anyway ... or at least that's what this callow 15-year-old made of it.

But it was a handy concept for someone who had no idea who he was or what he was and, to be honest, has never quite worked it out to this day. Back then there was no career guidance and, in truth, when it came to third level, the whole university thing seemed such an elitist activity. University fees limited admission to a tiny minority, and there was nothing about that minority that appealed to me.

Without much actual evidence, it seemed to me that all the students were culchies (yes, me, hardly a generation up from the country). I had no interest in rugby and even less in the GAA. My interests lay in buying and selling horses and hunting several days a week with a mate of mine, Leslie Fitzpatrick, an international showjumper.

My father wanted me to be a scientist. My mother wanted me to be a lawyer. I wanted to be a layabout. I won – or thought I did. If they said black, I said white. If they said it was raining, I said the sun was shining.

My greatest regret about my father is that I was not more interested in the things that fascinated him – which, ironically, were the same things that came to fascinate me as I grew older. I regret that I didn't know him better and was so arrogant and intolerant. But I didn't know what understanding was. I have apologised to him many times in my head.

He was passionate about education and felt a duty of care to the sciences. So, naturally, he assumed that his son would make a very good scientist. I believe my mother pleaded with him to let me take a year or two out to work, to knock the corners off me, and then send me off to university. Though her writ usually ran in the house, she lost that cause.

One year on the science degree course in UCD was enough to confirm she was right. I'm sure they both despaired.

There was a consequence for this 19-year-old, both then and far in the future, when I would have reason to do a lot of self-searching. But right then my problem was the lack of good layabout role models in the 1950s for me to 'aspire' to. Choices had to be made. You needed money, like everyone else – probably more of it, in view of the evolving lifestyle – but how did one accumulate it?

This was the challenge for a lad with absolutely no purpose in life except to chase women and drink and therefore in need of an income well above his station. I supposed then that I must be a businessman.

*

It was not a scenario that would have sat well in any sense with Marian's family, now or then. Farmers, shopkeepers, schoolteachers and Roman Catholics to the core of their being, they were rooted in Ballydesmond, an area of west Limerick on the Kerry border.

Her grandfather was the principal of Ballydesmond national school, a tough, hard man and dedicated teacher. Every year the master – as male principals were called then – picked the five brightest boys from poor families and prepared them for the British civil service exam. At 5 p.m.

every evening the master returned to give special evening classes for those boys. His purpose was not to provide servants of the empire – that was a side effect – but to give the boys a rare route out of poverty.

Thus prepared, five boys who had never been outside the village were each provided with a suit to wear and dispatched to London via the Ballydesmond network. Somebody from Ballydesmond would be waiting for the train at Westland Row station to escort them to the Liverpool ferry. In Liverpool, they were met by another Ballydesmond native, who would accompany them to the exam venue in London. The same network delivered them safely to each point on the return journey. Back in Ballydesmond, the five suits were returned and carefully stored for the next year's chosen five.

When the boys landed those permanent, pensionable jobs as civil servants with the British government, as they usually did, they reimbursed the master for the bus, train and boat fares. That was how he funded the programme.

The system did not reward such dedication. When the master, Marian's maternal grandfather, died suddenly in his forties, the family income died with him. There was no such thing as a widow's pension, nor was there much sensitivity about it either. 'It'll be the poorhouse for you lot,' someone was heard to say to the widow and mother of four young daughters at the funeral.

It was something else we had in common. Both our grandparents' generations had experienced the sudden, early death of the breadwinner, which led to a radical redrawing of their children's lives. But those tragedies were handled in very different ways.

Maura, the master's eldest child and Marian's mother in a future time, assumed the duty of rearing her siblings. When she got her teaching degree, every penny she earned went to supporting the family. They all achieved a secondary education before migrating to Dublin and availing of the few choices available to women: nun, teacher or housewife.

By the time Maura married Daniel Finucane and had her own children – Therese, Dorothy, Noel, Tomás and the youngest, Mary Catherine Marian, born in February 1950 – Maura had already raised another family. The funeral whispers of the poorhouse could have destroyed others. For the master's children, it was what drove them on. In one way or another, they all became educators fuelled by a sense of social justice.

Maura's sister Nora became a teacher and, more than that, a central figure in the founding of the Irish credit union movement. Teaching at an Irish Sisters of Charity school in Dublin during the 1950s, she was appalled at the effects of poverty, unemployment and the vicious cycle of money-lending on local families.

With an economics student, Thomas Hogan, she set up the Dublin Central Co-Operative Society, a workers' co-op, and then expanded her vision by travelling to study the Canadian Credit Union National Association model, designed for people too poor to have a bank account. Seán Lemass appointed her to an advisory committee on non-agricultural co-ops, and the first two Irish credit unions were formed in 1958. Her first employee was a young Derry lad called John Hume.

Nora lived like a hermit. She smoked like a train and dined almost exclusively on Vienna rolls, despite the family's best efforts to vary her diet. She also set up and ran the Irish League of Credit Unions, unpaid, from her Dublin living room, teaching full-time and funding its development with her earnings. Her contribution was recognised when she stood beside President Éamon de Valera as he signed the 1966 Credit Union Act into law.

This was the solid social-justice ethos in which Marian was raised.

She was 12 when her father, Daniel, a garda sergeant, died at only 55. For the last five years of his life, a heart condition meant he could only work in the afternoons, and Marian's frequent throat infections meant she was at home quite a lot. As a result, they became very close. She loved that time with him, sitting at the end of his bed listening to his stories about history, current affairs and how world events evolve. Like Marian, he read widely and voraciously, and though he wasn't formally educated, she always said he was one of the most educated men she had ever known.

Marian often referred to the incident when Maura arrived in, appalled, to find him reading the Bible. 'Great God, Dan, you'll lose your immortal soul if you read that book.' In that Ireland, ordinary people could not be trusted to read the Bible without the supervision of an informed person, apparently.

That incident spurred her to get her hands on every book she wasn't supposed to read. Daniel's influence on Marian was profound. 'Straighten your back, walk tall, keep walking tall,' he used to say to his tall girl.

She always did.

His death was one of those subjects that went into the depths of the iceberg, the first of several catastrophic events in her life that were never up for discussion. It was her way of coping. But they were never forgotten. They went round and round in secret compartments, were taken out, examined, looked at and put back in again. And they were hers – her privacy, her no-go areas.

During all that time, Maura hauled Marian and the others out to seven o'clock Mass, came home, gave them breakfast, raced into Phibsborough school, where she taught at the time, raced home at lunchtime and gave them lunch.

Then she drove Daniel to work. And when he died, Maura was left alone again to carry the responsibility for her family, sustained by her teaching job, her faith and the heavy responsibility of giving her five children the best chance she could in life. She was a remarkable woman who undoubtedly had private questions of her own about her beloved Church.

It was Maura who told the story about a class of children she had prepared for Confirmation and who were all lined up in their pews, dressed in their very best, when Archbishop John Charles McQuaid arrived to confer his blessing. 'Which is the illegitimate child?' he asked. He then proceeded to put the routine doctrinal questions to each young Confirmation candidate, except the illegitimate child, whom he pointedly ignored. The incident shocked Maura, a card-carrying Catholic, to her soul. On countless occasions throughout her life, Marian would bring it up and say, 'How could a human being do that to a child?'

As an institution, the Catholic Church was capable of astonishing cruelty, yet there were always individuals within it working quietly to undo the harm. Marian found some of them in an institution that would prove to be another major influence on her life. Though chosen for its excellent exam results, Scoil Chaitríona, an all-Irish secondary school in Glasnevin run by the Dominican nuns, was well ahead of its time in its promotion of independent-minded women.

Many years later, Marian still recalled that moment when the reverend mother told the newly arrived girls, 'You are all here to find out how to ask a question, not to get an answer' – adding that, if need be, the girls were to question the nuns too. The idea of an authority figure like a nun inviting questions from a girl was radical for the time and, I believe, was pivotal in Marian's development. She also fondly remembered an Irish teacher who raised current affairs and civil rights in class and built on the curiosity first stirred by Marian's conversations with her father.

To see girls being taught to believe that everything was up for questioning, and they could do anything they set their minds on, was quite mind-blowing for a convent schoolgirl in the 1960s. That was the forum where the shy young Marian could find her public voice, where her formidable debating skills were sparked and nurtured and where she got a sense of her skill at engaging an audience. As well as that, students were taught entirely through Irish, the language that Marian embraced and encouraged all her life. It was also perceived to give them an edge in the debating forum.

Marian also flourished academically in Scoil Chaitríona. She was only 16 when she achieved an all-honours Leaving Certificate and was considered too young for third level. When she repeated the year at St Louis convent boarding school in Monaghan – where Nuala O'Faolain also happened to be a pupil – she achieved full honours the second time around, one of just a handful of girls encouraged to believe they could aspire to and succeed at honours maths in the Leaving Cert.

*

I did honours maths in the Leaving too, but with fewer fireworks. If you broke the 40 per cent mark in St Conleth's, you were considered a bloody genius. I was good at numeracy but poor on theory. Marian was appalling on numeracy but brilliant on the theoretical aspect of honours maths. She once told me she liked the subject because it was about probabilities, not certainties. Certainties were too easy for her.

As she grew in confidence and into the rackety world around her, the nuances would become the places where she preferred to live. I believe she always had a quiet thought-gestation period, which might last five years, one year, one week or one hour. And then out of the blue, she would make a statement or give an opinion of some kind and you'd wonder, 'Was she actually thinking of that for the last five years?'

She brought that mindset into her journalism and her judgement, into almost everything she did.

By contrast, I was into the laws of chaos – obviously, many might say – a school of thinking that hadn't a vast following then or now. It roughly states that our very being is random, whether we live or die is random, and our certainties are illusory. Hence our fears and endless search for identity and security, God and religion are just substitutes for the uncertainties. It would drive her mad – but that was a few years away still.

Marian was stepping out in the world at a time of extraordinary generational flux – 1968 would become the iconic year of global protest, and she was primed. A generational divide was slowly evolving. Her family remained conventional card-carrying Catholics. The daily Mass-going remained mandatory as long as she was living at home.

But an abyss was beginning to open up between the youngest and the rest of the family. They remained close to the end but could never know what Marian was really thinking or reading or getting up to. Most people couldn't. I'm not too sure if she knew herself. In that sense, she may not have been all that different from every other 18- or 19-year-old of that generation. That famously impenetrable reserve of the public broadcaster was not merely an expression of the necessary professional impartiality nor a protective buffer from the public; below the surface of the iceberg, there was a slow, deeply painful process of detachment from many of the tenets she had grown up with. Not least of these was the Catholic Church, a kind of estrangement that would grow into a discreet but uncompromising anger and suspicion of all its works and representatives.

Her grandmother, the master's widow, lived to the age of 99, chain-smoking Woodbines to the end.

TWO

A Businessman?

My father had no idea what I was talking about when I told him what I wanted to be. 'A businessman?'

For people of his class and generation in Ireland, business meant a job in the bank or a stockbroker's or in Arthur Guinness's. The other things that some called 'business' seemed to them to be quite seedy and odd, and the people involved were bound to be up to some shady trickery.

Yet there was a whole other kind of business going on, a world away from my father's. It was just hard to put a name to it.

But lo, I was finding my tribe. As far as I could see, business was all about making a few bob and having a drink. I was full of ideas and found it easy to make money. My mother excelled at numeracy and she and I dabbled in art, antiques and property. So that's what I did, and I took to it like a duck to water.

*

My first proper job was selling plaster to builders' merchants. Aodogán O'Rahilly, best known as the boy whose father was killed in the Easter Rising, owned gypsum mines in Cavan and had grown wealthy manufacturing tiles and plasterboard. So the 19-year-old commercial me – not the auld existentialist one, obviously – proceeded to travel around Ireland selling tonnes of it. Aodogán was one of the first people I encountered in those early years with a vision for native industry.

But whatever I was up to otherwise, it was nothing good as far as my mother could see. The boat to England was a rite of passage for most Irish people, but the nudge came from her.

A few things aligned. I had a talent for buying or selling anything and was making a few pounds here and there but clearly not enough to fund my lifestyle. At some point the manager of the Ulster Bank in Ranelagh – also my father's bank – wrote to say I was overdrawn and would I come in at once. Me being me, I didn't take kindly to the patriarchal lecture about living within one's means. Call it petty, but I promised myself that I would always earn more than a bank manager. The master's family in Ballydesmond might have been driven by threats of the poorhouse, but for this 21-year-old it was about never having to be talked down to about money again. Make what you will of that.

Ultimately, my mother's hope was that England might temper some of my wildness while providing gainful employment.

The upside of the plan was that my aunt Una was there – one of UCD's first gold medallists in English, a product of Granny Cosgrove's feminist vision – whom I adored.

*

On my first Holyhead boat crossing, a trail of tears for generations of Irish emigrants, I witnessed a scene that left an indelible mark on this feckless youth.

At the British customs checkpoint, which was still operating on a quasi-wartime footing in 1957, all passengers were required to open their bags for inspection. Next to me in line was a young woman in her early twenties, lugging a suitcase made of some kind of brown cardboard fibre.

I opened my case. It contained a suit, shirts, trousers, some ties, underwear – all the appropriate apparel for an aspiring young businessman. Then the young woman opened hers. It contained a bunch of daffodils. Nothing else. All she had was what she stood up in. Back at home, or somewhere on the way to the boat, she had stopped to pick daffodils as a keepsake, maybe, or to bring as a gift to an aunt or relative in England. I was stunned.

Everything about that woman and her daffodils articulated all anyone needed to know about the Ireland of the 1950s. To this day it haunts and angers me.

I was an angry young man anyway, despite my privilege. Catholic-ridden Ireland was no place for me, the supposed intellectual. I was angry about having to go to England, angry that even if I had particular skills there was nowhere here to use them. There was little outlet for entrepreneurship that I could see.

The economy was in freefall and emigration was soaring. Growth rates were stuck at 1 per cent and 43,000 people were emigrating a year. The decade was characterised by austerity, massive emigration, near bankruptcy and political instability. And a mindset of dependency. And still the primary political objective, believe it or not, was the reunification of the country.

We were clinging to a vast protective barrier of tariffs, basically a protectionist blockade. Our economic policy amounted to gross national self-sabotage. When I took the boat, the famous Programme for Economic

Expansion conceived by the new 39-year-old secretary of the Department of Finance, Dr Ken Whitaker, to harry the country into a competitive, free-trading nation was still a year away.

In a near perfect reflection of the national stasis, a 75-year-old, almost blind and increasingly remote Éamon de Valera had just been re-elected Taoiseach, still ruling his cabinet by dint of civil war loyalty and adulation for 'The Chief'. Whitaker could see the big picture. De Valera, as Whitaker succinctly put it, was 'a symbol of Éire passé'.

But as Whitaker predicted, it would be a long, slow evolution. School texts had conditioned us to believe that Ireland had no natural resources. In fact, we had a huge one: it was called humans. But they were not perceived as such. We squandered them, saw them as a liability and shipped them out.

Many years later, Marian and I went to Ellis Island in New York and felt the poignancy of all those Irish names, impoverished and desperate, who had come through it. The occupations listed for the endless stream of Irish immigrants from, say, 1900 were 'labourer', 'labourer', 'labourer', 'housemaid', 'housemaid' ... That was the only asset we carried: our sweat. The Italians were much the same. The English were listed as 'gentleman', 'plumber', 'soldier of fortune', as were the Germans. As soon as the Irish shook off the shackles of theocracy, the notions of respectability or getting above their station, many of them prospered. We were fascinated with those indicators of how society moved and shifted towards the tipping points.

Other factors were working against us then. Decades before, under British rule, virtually all industry on the island had been moved up to the Northern enclave, no doubt with a wary eye on the new confident nationalism arising from the cultural renaissance in art, literature and sport. Shipbuilding, rope manufacturing, cotton and flax industries had all gone north. Barry's of Cork had to import all their tea through the port of Belfast.

Industry was not part of the mindset here. Parliamentarians of the new Free State were drawn from farmers, publicans, teachers and lawyers and were otherwise occupied trying to maintain democracy and establish a state. Most civil servants came from small farming backgrounds and were bright enough to win scholarships but had no idea how factories worked. There was little concept of entrepreneurship or industry.

The powers that be saw the ethos of the nation as the farmer with the donkey and cart and two churns of milk on the back heading for the creamery. It took an agonisingly long time for them to see that by combining all three you had an industry.

This was the Ireland of the young woman bound for England with nothing but daffodils in her cardboard suitcase.

*

I was lucky that Aunt Una had a highly flattering view of my qualifications. She spotted an advertisement for an analytical chemist in what she took to be a sugar company in Blackwall Tunnel – a daring move for a 21-year-old with one year of indifferent science. Luckily the job turned out to be manageable for someone with a rudimentary knowledge of chemistry. The company made glucose for a new drink on the market called Lucozade, then being sold into hospitals by the truck load. The structural flaw in the processing was that the batches often emerged in different colours, which was not acceptable to the home market. So, what did they do? They exported them instead. Just like that.

To me, this seemed amazing. British industry casually perceived the world as their market. Back in Ireland, we were still selling our cattle on the hoof, driving them down the North Circular Road and onto the boats, because a slaughter industry was in no one's vision.

Whatever Ireland's many flaws and failings, however, England was quickly losing any charm it had for this wild rover. The gainful employment was there but I was eaten up with loneliness. Home in London was a bedsit run by two quintessential old landladies who happened to be sisters of Ivor Novello – the Welsh singer and songwriter of 'Keep the Home Fires Burning' fame – which was of no assistance to a young Irish lad who didn't know that vast city, had no mentor to advise him and was feeling desperately isolated.

The social spots of Cricklewood were not for me. Aunt Una suggested the Irish Club in Eaton Square – but all I could think of was the jars with the lads, the craic, the mad, meandering conversations of home. I wanted Dublin.

I lasted about a year in London. The problem then was that when I returned to Ireland, I brought the wildness back with me.

It was 1958 and I needed a job.

*

Like almost everything in life, it happened on a random encounter.

A ladies' clothes manufacturer called Lenny Jacobs told me about an English company which had invented a revolutionary adhesive interlining that was modernising production lines and changing the face of the garment industry. My job was to sell this amazing new product to Irish clothing manufacturers. The really attractive part was that the job required trips to Europe and, even better, flights to London every Friday for conferences. We were moving into the Swinging Sixties. For a few spectacular, crazy years, I swung.

A few young architects had fled to Ireland, in case they were called up by the army, and worked for Arthur Gibney, returning to London when everything settled down. Bill Siddons became a friend and was now on the cutting edge of London celebrity, designing shopfronts and working for a sir who slept under a couch in his office with an owl and was a mate of Anthony Armstrong-Jones, who was walking out with Princess Margaret. On Friday nights, Bill would have a list of anything-goes parties for our pleasure.

I was delighted with myself, in my mid-twenties and money flowing in. The problem – as always – was that it flowed out just as fast. I was drinking a lot, but so was everyone else, as far as I could see. And I was investing in property, even if the banks were unable to see mountains in Mayo as a profitable idea for their money.

The mountain land in North Mayo was being thrown

away at £1 an acre. I bought several thousand acres and suddenly realised there were no people there. The whole of Ballycroy had been devastated by emigration.

My sister Elizabeth, who was very unsettled working in the RDS, saw the mountains as an escape from her life. She asked me to buy her a farm. I had bought two deserted farms in Mayo that week at £500 each. She paid me for one, packed up her Volkswagen Beetle, disappeared to the mountain in North Mayo and never left.

She married Pakie Walsh, a shepherd with a flock on Nephin Beg, and together they built up a sheep farm on over a thousand acres of mountain. Elizabeth was an extraordinary woman who could build barns and castrate cattle. She and Pakie had three children, each with their own surprising story, one becoming the vice-president of marketing in an international hotel chain.

Other money-making schemes of mine didn't work out as well as the mountain. A plan to get a highly profitable Swedish weaving company to take over the ailing Irish tweed industry looked hopeful for a while – and would have yielded a healthy, much-needed commission for me – but fell through when word came back that the Scandinavian managers and senior weavers were not falling over themselves to come and work in Ireland.

One way or another, a clothing sector built behind tariff walls could never survive in the hot furnace of competition that came with the opening up of markets to the EEC in the 1970s. The textile industry died rather suddenly, and 35,000 jobs died with it. Its vanishing felt like a disaster for places in the inner city, where kids couldn't wait to reach 14 to get into the rag trade and start earning.

Yet even as the rag trade died, 14-year-olds were raising their sights to state exams like the Inter Cert. Donogh O'Malley's extraordinary solo run in declaring free education up to the Intermediate Certificate had kick-started the erosion of the rigid, sharply defined class system of the 1950s and gave working-class children a fighting chance of getting a Leaving Cert and perhaps making it into third level. So the kids were no longer available for cheap labour. Industries needed to operate on much larger margins to afford the level of wages that those young people were entitled to for their work.

But at its height, through the worst of times, the rag trade supported 35,000 Irish workers in one way or another, including me.

Ireland was stirring, beginning to morph and change, and I was in the middle of it. Did I see it? I would be lying if I said so. But the whirring in the undergrowth of industry and politics was almost palpable. Like them or not, we had youngsters like Charlie Haughey and Donogh O'Malley in politics and visionaries like Seán Lemass, T.K. Whitaker and Mickey Joe Costello, who had an understanding of business and investment and were figuring out how to push out the old brigade. Whitaker's support of innovative and evidence-based thinking was paying off. Emigration rates came down and the population was growing with the economy.

Within that weft of change and industry in the new economy, the IDA and Córas Tráchtála were the two pillars with the job of enticing foreign inward investment and supporting and developing exporters. The Irish Management Institute was also playing a key role in educating future leaders. It gave confidence to the would-be entrepreneurs. The fashion industry and Sybil Connolly were getting involved and gave a glamorous edge to exporting stuff.

*

It was around then that Arthur Gibney and I fell across each other.

We first met in a pub. Obviously. Brian's in Molesworth Street – later reincarnated as the passport office – was the alternative intellectuals' pub, the ones who were drawn to a different way of thinking, as we liked to believe, hovering between industrial quantities of hot air, the price of a pint and *The Decline of the West* – Spengler's upending of the Eurocentric view of history, which I had made a point of reading.

Arthur and I were from completely different backgrounds, but we were in the same boat, hunting around for business. He and Sam Stephenson, the entrepreneurial partner in their architectural enterprise, were the new bloods on the block, with glamorous offices above Brown Thomas, ready to take on anyone and any project.

Sam's father was the chief librarian of Dublin. Arthur's father, a dentist, had died when he was relatively young, and Arthur began his working life as a clerk in Dublin Shipping. But his talent for painting of all genres won him several scholarships, including the prestigious RDS Taylor Art Award, and during a trip to Italy, he decided to sign up to the Bolton Street School of Architecture, where he met Sam.

The pair joined forces in 1960, the go-to firm for the groundbreaking architecture that came to epitomise the Ireland of the era and cemented the idea of Bolton Street as a cradle of daring architectural innovation.

They designed contentious new buildings in the style

of Mies van der Rohe and Bauhaus, sometimes on the sites of even more contentious demolitions that became the focus of large protests – protests that would later include a vocal young one called Marian Finucane. I was dabbling in property myself. Developers were building up the suburbs, where planning was a joke, while property in the city was being left to rot and becoming available for almost nothing. I bought a few houses and converted them into flats. Great work for an entrepreneur – except I was no entrepreneur. The money I made was devoted to maintaining the nice lifestyle to which I was accustomed, which included frequent visits to the famous and expensive Jammet's restaurant and a range of pubs around Grafton Street and environs where Arthur and I would discourse at great length.

When he married Phyllis, a stained-glass artist, she would often be there in the pub with him, silent, reading a book, while whole subsets of dissidents, creatives, opportunists and philosopher drunks swayed in and out of each other's circles.

One lot resented the centrality of religion and the influence of priests. There was a gamblers' lot and a philosophers' circle and an older coterie of artists, writers and erstwhile republicans that gathered in McDaid's in

Harry Street and often resorted to the Catacombs for after-hours drinking, a kind of síbín in a Fitzwilliam Square basement. The company included people like Brendan Behan, Anthony Cronin and a compatriot of the author J. P. Donleavy's, Gainor Crist, who was the inspiration for Sebastian Dangerfield in Donleavy's fantastically successful novel *The Ginger Man*, described by Dorothy Parker as 'a rigadoon of rascality, a bawled-out comic song of sex'. It fell foul of the censorship lords and was banned in Ireland for 20 years. When it was adapted to the stage, it closed after three nights, following an approach to the Gaiety management by a representative of our old friend, the Archbishop of Dublin, John Charles McQuaid.

I was interested in art in all its forms and enjoyed encounters with men such as Behan's father-in-law, Cecil Salkeld, Harry Kernoff, who sold his paintings for a fiver at the time, and Sean O'Sullivan.

Gibney had a particularly eclectic set of acquaintances. He was very close to Brendan Behan and knew another set of squatters in a house down in Sheriff Street who read the most esoteric philosophy. All were part of a series of little groups who didn't feel they fitted into Dublin at all. In a way, it was Ireland's contribution to the global age of dissent.

We comprised our own little subset. Lads with money, lads trying to make money, lads who drank epic amounts of alcohol, stayed out till the late hours on 'business' and went home to wives who had probably given up asking where they had been. A subset of the lads generally derided by the media as 'the mohair suit brigade', lampooned in a 1969 book by Alan Bestic, *The Importance of Being Irish*, as 'unhappy people with easy laughs and eyes that are always moving, looking for Murphy, wondering whether he is watching and whether he has a mohair suit too ... blurred carbons of English suburbans from the mock stockbroker belt'.

Not entirely inaccurate, I would say.

By now I was working in Irish International, the advertising business founded by businessman Tim O'Neill, and had married his daughter, Catherine. He had done a merger with an English company and, for once, my misspent youth proved useful. My book of contacts helped to build up the business with contemporaries and blue-chip clients like Findus, Penneys and Jacobs.

My plan to be a North Mayo sheep farmer was upended when Catherine took one look at the mountain and said, 'You must be joking.' She was a city girl and a realist.

So it became a dual existence. I was a sheep farmer who also worked in advertising and wore mohair suits. The fact that most of the western world wore the same suits in those years seemed to elude the critics. Our lot were characterised as gangsters, chancers, fibbers, fellas on the make, getting above their station with their choice of clothes. By those lights, industry then was only for our betters, for other people. The fellas in the mohair suits, the Johnny-come-latelys? No, not for them.

Odd as it seems now, the mohair suits were probably among the rebels then, brash and arrogant, moving between the cliques of the establishment, the politicians, the hierarchy, the numerous overlapping circles who found much to dislike about Irish society, and then out to the ordinary, decent strivers trying to make a living. This was all part of the birth pangs of change I was witnessing. The challenge for them was to touch base with those different groups regularly.

But there were two major organisations in Irish society that all of these groups had to contend with: the Freemasons on the one hand and the Knights of St Columbanus on the other. Their influence was incalculable. Most importantly, they had the final say in who got the top jobs in their sphere of influence. While the state-mandated culture was Catholic, the same rules applied with equal rigidity where certain old businesses were still resolutely Protestant-led.

When my friend Dick Frost – whose father was an Englishman who went to Ampleforth and Trinity College, then became managing director of Shell Far East and, by the way, was a Roman Catholic – got a job in Guinness's, he was told by his boss straight out that he would never get to the top of the ladder in the Protestant-led company because he was a Catholic. Dick never aspired to climb any ladder, but he knew the lie of the land. RTÉ was mostly a creature of the Knights of Columbanus. It was either that or the Stickies, a Sinn Féin spin-off, hardline, socialist group, nicknamed for the adhesive versions of the Easter lily badge.

This was the Dublin of Archbishop John Charles McQuaid and a time when every politician skidded to his knees when he saw the ring of a bishop, and nobody dared to step outside that. That was how it was and people could rail against it, game it or just ignore it.

This tiny place somehow hosted all these disparate groups of people, many of them struggling to climb out from under the cloak of McQuaid and Irish respectability. That was the Dublin that Gibney and I knocked around in. We were a very unsettled, fairly uncouth lot.

But I was young then and maybe I felt the world was mine.

*

The rebuilders of Dublin were on the rampage, for good or ill. Vatican II had taken the edge off the theocratic state, and the bishops began to recognise the limits of their moral and political influence. Education was changing the face of Ireland. The women's liberation movement was crashing into the public consciousness, and artificial contraception was the first item on the agenda.

We became part of something called the common market.

Revolutions that have no violence are sometimes very hard to see. But I could sense it. Time to let the go-getters get on with it. Make way for the mohair suits or – as some would have it – the jackals.

There was money to be made.

Arthur Gibney and Sam Stephenson were in the thick of it. At a time when most of their peers had to emigrate for lack of work, they were leading the charge on the old-school firms who designed churches and red-brick buildings. Between them, they set the pace for the next 20 years, wheeling and dealing, inventing new ways to play the game, kicking out at convention.

And somewhere out there a young Marian Finucane was on the march, asking the kind of questions that would occupy the two of us, and soon the whole country, for nearly fifty years.

Eventually all those circles would overlap and lead her to the doorstep of Stephenson Gibney, and I would be standing there.

THREE

Marian, Meantime

Young Finucane's first television appearance, cleaning the doorposts of a Georgian house in Christmas week 1970, was a useful signpost to her character and future calling.

She was among a group of protestors and occupiers – mainly young architecture students – who put a sudden stop to demolition work on rows of Georgian houses in what became known as the Battle for Hume Street.

Always a very shy woman, it was her passion for Georgian Dublin that motivated her to stand in front of the cameras when RTÉ's Patrick Gallagher called in for a look around and a vox pop. Speaking calmly, carefully and clearly, she was the ideal television interviewee, explaining how she felt it was her responsibility as an architecture student 'being helped along by the taxpayer', and as a Dubliner, to ensure the houses were not demolished.

Their efforts hadn't come from a vacuum. They were tapping into an anger generated by a previous notorious demolition, when 16 centuries-old Georgian houses, part of the longest Georgian streetscape in existence, were cleared for a new ESB headquarters in Lower Fitzwilliam Street.

The political mood of the times was governed by a single imperative: to obliterate any trace of British culture. We had a culture war at least half a century before Silicon Valley was ever heard of.

And it was a classic. The minister for local government, staunch republican Kevin Boland, summarised one side memorably when he characterised the Irish Georgian Society as 'a consortium of belted earls ... I make no apology for saying that the physical needs of the people may get priority over the aesthetic needs of Lord and Lady Guinness.' Seán Lemass declared himself 'a complete modernist' and told the Dáil, 'we have enough museum pieces without looking for more'.

Dublin was being remodelled, reshaped, knocked down. Finucane was taking note, questioning the old shapes of how society worked, starting to ask questions about the institutions and authorities and those who ran them and how their decisions were shaping up for the people around her.

The Green Property Company was already buying up much of Hume Street when the street was listed for preservation in the first Dublin draft development plan. The company's first application to clear a site for office blocks was refused, but Boland gave it the go-ahead.

Demolition began and the students took over. It became a huge cause célèbre. People visited from all over the country, and international voices chimed in. School groups came on tour, and some returned to help with the cleaning work. A lot of the occupiers' time was spent showing people around, promoting the cause. During the months of protest and occupation of one of the houses, the occupiers and helpers engaged in serious repair work, cleaning, restoring floors, reassembling old marble mantelpieces. The staircase had been ripped out, so the battle plan, in the event of a raid, was to retreat to the upper floors via a ladder, which could then be raised.

Since the media was paying close attention by now, so were the politicians.

Charlie Haughey, minister for finance up to a few months previously and personification of the men in mohair suits, sent word to the Shelbourne hotel to make showers available for the occupiers and ordered a Christmas hamper to be sent around to them. Some rejected the offering as a blatant attempt at right-wing bribery. For Finucane, the hamper represented an agony of temptation. She had run out of cigarettes and knew there were two packs inside. There followed a marathon debate, I believe, about whether the cigarettes should be smoked. I couldn't possibly comment.

A month after the occupation began, the minister for justice, Dessie O'Malley, introduced the second stage of the Prohibition of Forcible Entry and Occupation Bill 1970, aimed at squatters generally and at the Hume Street occupiers in particular.

Tom Fitzpatrick, a senior Fine Gael TD and qualified solicitor, put the case for the defence while giving a sense of a cultural shift. He described how the students and others demonstrated 'first peacefully and eventually in an unlawful manner, to publicise the fact that Georgian houses in Dublin were being demolished, were to be replaced by modern office blocks and the city of Dublin thereby was to be robbed of its character. These people had a legitimate and understandable point of view,' he told the Dáil. 'They protested in a peaceable and orderly manner for many months. They sought to convince the powers that be that it was wrong to pull down these houses and that a great number of people in the city and throughout the country favoured the retention of these houses ... They did that in a lawful way until they were blue in the face.' No one would listen to them, he said – indeed, the government through the minister for local government had 'insulted the protestors and those who agreed with them by describing them as "belted earls" and ... expressed his utter contempt for them and all that they stood for'.

When the protestors 'were driven to unlawful means, to forcible entry, to unlawful squatting, the government climbed down', said Fitzpatrick. Assurances were given that the houses would stand, he said. 'Lawful efforts failed but unlawful efforts prevailed.'

They did not prevail, as it happened. The development got the go-ahead provided the façades of the original houses were, not retained, just reproduced. But no one could deny that the students and leaders had won a huge moral victory. By aligning themselves with the very few preservation stalwarts of the Georgian Society and others, they contributed hugely to raising awareness of Dublin's heritage and gave the lie to those who dismissed conservationists as outsiders. Conservation became everyone's business. That was the kind of outcome that always made Finucane's heart soar.

*

There was a certain irony to all this for me, since architects such as my friends at Stephenson Gibney were among the more conspicuous beneficiaries of the demolitions, ready to grab any commission that was going. When the ESB put the design for its new headquarters on Lower Fitzwilliam Street out to competition, it was Stephenson Gibney that won the day. But Finucane's passion for conservation never altered her view of them as the best architects in town.

She was coming from the Bolton Street School of Architecture, which carried its reputation for the bright, the new and the cutting edge before it, courtesy of the Stephenson Gibney generation. For some, its main appeal was that it was not UCD, then perceived to be stuck in the comfortable old-school groove of traditional good taste, patronage and connections, under Professor Desmond FitzGerald.

Bolton Street, by contrast, was the scrappy young underdog, lodged in the north inner city, for socially mobile young ones hungry for work and hungry for design. It was perceived as a more practical, less academic education, attracting a more dynamic range of youngsters into the business and making them more immediately employable. In a world where connections got you everywhere, a new, more equitable system meant that big development projects were being put out to public competition. Enter the Bolton Street kids who never had the privilege of wealthy connections or patrons. Now their work was up there for public scrutiny with the same chance, in theory, as everyone else.

The underdog mentality was fuelled by stories such as the one about a UCD students' union party held in the Casino Marino. When some invited Bolton Street students turned up, the door was opened by Professor FitzGerald. 'We're from Bolton Street,' said the fellow in front by way of explanation. 'I don't care what street you're from, you're not coming in here,' said the professor, allegedly.

But Bolton Street had its own set of challenges in that era.

Marian was among only three or four women in a class of 30, and misogyny was on open display from a couple of lecturers in particular. One was a man who thought women had no business there in the first place. Another was markedly more abrasive with the female students when projects were being critiqued in class.

Apart from the marches and sit-ins, Marian's college years were tame by student standards. When the group went to New York for the J1 summer of 1969, the year before we met, she got a job in Columbia University and stayed with her aunt in Brooklyn. The rest of the gang had an apartment in Manhattan.

There's no doubt that the debating society was her refuge and her strength, combining two of her great interests – communication skills and current affairs.

The society was moribund when John McCrossan and others arrived in 1966. Fortunately for Marian, they had managed to resuscitate it by the time she arrived the following year. The group gelled into a tight half-dozen, keen to broaden their education and very serious about their reading matter. All of them, including Marian, were conscious that in loftier circles colleges of technology were dismissed as 'techs' and not taken very seriously. That perception of themselves as underdogs and outsiders fired them up to fight harder so they wouldn't make a show of themselves against the elite universities.

That spur was more keenly felt when they entered the *Irish Times* debating competition. 'We're not going there to learn something,' Marian would say. 'We're going to go in there to debate with these people on their own level.'

Apart from being a serious, competitive pursuit for the participants – who were taken very seriously, for the main part, and took themselves very seriously – the debates attracted huge, highly engaged audiences. Ireland was on the cusp of massive social and political change. Many were leaving the Church behind. Politics was a major topic, and for many the debates were the only source of intelligent conversation and social gathering outside of student politics and the rugger buggers.

The Friday-night debates packed out the Kinema, the Bolton Street auditorium. When UCD's Literary and Historical Society hosted a debate on Vietnam with the then US ambassador, students queued all the way around Earlsfort Terrace. The Sunday papers carried prominent reports.

Finucane was a superb speaker. Though incredibly shy, once she began to speak, she soared. She could instantly engage an audience, think on her feet and deviate from a point if the mood took her, and she proved well able to swat away the hecklers. She loved the frisson and standing up in places like the unruly bearpit of UCD with the sense that anything could happen during a live event. It was a preview of what drove her in broadcasting. In later years, I could see she liked nothing more than a live broadcast, a time when she lived on her nerves.

She and Noel Kidney twice made the final of the *Irish Times* debating competition, to general amazement. When she won the best individual speaker award, the first woman to win that coveted title, Adrian Hardiman, her opposition – a repeat winner, future senior counsel and supreme court judge – was openly incredulous at this massive and massively unlikely triumph for the tech kids. He turned around to Marian, saying, 'There has to be some mistake,' and demanded a judges' recheck. She was most definitely not amused at the time, although we all became close friends in later years. When she took libel actions against some of the papers, it was Adrian she chose to be her counsel.

Coming second in the highly prestigious Observer Mace debate at the Oxford Union cut her to the quick. She was still self-flagellating about it years later, mainly because she felt she let it get away. Her suspicions were confirmed at the post-debate dinner. She was holding forth on some topic when one of the judges looked at her quizzically and said – I paraphrase – 'If you'd talked like that at the debate, you would have walked away with it.'

So what had happened to her? She was a visitor, and they were from Oxford and Cambridge: it was just her damned Celtic inhibitions, she reckoned, after giving it some thought. The judge's words were salt in the wound but a pivotal moment for broadcasting. She knew now that she could do it.

She and I had become involved by then. After the year

out at Stephenson Gibney, she had returned to Bolton St and large-scale disenchantment was setting in. Her old group had moved on. And by the end of the year so would she.

FOUR

Breaking Up, Moving On

I married Catherine when I was 28 – not exactly a child, yet not mature enough to accept the constraints of married life or much else in 1964. The wildness and drinking that had worried my mother hadn't abated. I moved in circles where domestic schedules were low on the list.

My role model, I imagined, was my own father, a gentle, loving man who always believed that fathers should have more input with their children and enjoy them. By that yardstick, I felt I was spending plenty of time with our three kids, arriving home to help get them to bed. What actually happened was that I would leave some premises around nine, drive half-drunk, as many people did in those days, and say hello to the kids and the wife. Truth be told, I felt it was her job to mind the children and keep the house habitable.

As women's liberation began to shift the conversation around us, I was fully confident I knew more than most. I knew more about feminism, I reckoned, than any woman alive because I'd been raised by women who never sought permission to do anything. My mother, Sheila, ran an independent life, my father adored her, and her word was law in the household. It would never have crossed Granny Cosgrove's mind or Sheila's that they couldn't run a business or make decisions for themselves. Sheila was property dealing and playing the stock market when I was a child. I thought women were equal and their opinions were definitely their own and no one else's.

Yet I never questioned the idea that I should be the head of the household – or that it was the same for 99 per cent of people in our situation. It was a kind of dual thinking. Nuala O'Faolain's father was head of the household nominally. That didn't stop Nuala going to college or holding a job – but she still deferred to the man of the house. Perhaps it was a sort of transition stage in feminist travel.

I can only say that I was a man of my time. The marriage vows said love, honour and obey, and they were two separate units: her indoors, him outside. She indoors looked after the kids and the house, and he came back from time to time.

All of the above had to be reviewed much later, of course, when Finucane challenged it with a litany of facts. Did I know that at one stage, when her mother was a teacher and a widow with five children to support, there were three separate rates of pay – one for married men, one for single men and just one rate for all women, which was less than the pay for a single man? Did I know that a lot of women had to leave their jobs when they got married? Did I know about the laws that denied her autonomy over her own body? And that was just to start…

How did I not know all that? I have no idea. It would take me a while to absorb this new information, contrast it with what I knew and work out where I stood in it all. But from the day I left school, the immutable truth was that the male as head of household was the norm and it never crossed my mind to change. That was part of Catherine's and my misfortune.

The greater part was how that dovetailed neatly with my lifestyle. There was a drink culture and I was an enthusiastic participant. We applauded the capacity to be heavy drinkers and to be drunk while upright. Hemingway wrote about it. The last chap to fall off the barstool was the winner. Hard men, hard living. It was a handy prism for the lads to view life through.

Catherine was acquainted with that culture. Her father, Tim O'Neill, ran an advertising agency, and her family was accustomed to a culture of gin and tonics at 11 and a small glug of this and a little drop of that until you arrived at lunch and had a little more. It was how business was done, from my perspective, so my drinking probably wouldn't have been shocking to her or to many in that era. There was a strip of society here, in business and in politics, that was awash with drink.

Like others of the mohair-suit brigade, I was making a lot of money and spreading it around. Yet we were full of insecurities. It could hardly be otherwise. When Arthur Gibney's father died very young, his mother had trouble putting food on the table – now, suddenly, here he was in the big time, a focus of celebration, even adulation. The truth is we ran with fear, racing towards the next deal. People in permanent, pensionable jobs might have been surprised at the uncertainties these brash gamblers, entrepreneurs and chancers brought to the table. The existentialist part of me said, 'This is how society operates and I have to join it.'

I had a complex relationship with myself – and with women.

Did the prospect of an affair with a fun, clever, good-looking woman like Finucane tick every cliché in the book? You might think so. Yet there were plenty of clever, attractive women out there. True sexual liberation was still some way off, but there were casual affairs and flings among contemporaries, of course, and a lot of drunken groping at parties. But once I met Finucane, I lost interest in other women. Completely.

The chemistry between us was crazy but it was more than that.

I was very much in love with her and she was certainly in love with me.

*

Back in Bolton Street, following her year out, she was deeply unsettled. After the craic and the adrenaline of the marches and the sit-ins and the intoxication – literal and otherwise – of the Clarke–Gibney view of life, college was looking very stale and sober.

It felt like a different place with a different ethos, she said. The group she had started out with, the debaters, idealists and protestors who enjoyed a couple of pints over in the Bolton Horse, had moved on. She felt she would never be anything more than a competent designer and would never make it as an architect.

A chance meeting with John O'Donoghue from RTÉ had planted the idea of a presenter's job in her head, and for her, it felt like a switch had been flicked.

And there was also the matter of us. The passionate encounters and the enthralling conversations, the agony and the euphoria. We knew what we were doing was irresponsible, and she said we were courting disaster, breaking up families and hurting children. And something else: she had started seeing a man called Larry Granville, another architect, previously of Stephenson Gibney and now at Creedon's, where he had swung a job for her after her early exit from Bolton Street.

Her logic was inescapable. We agreed that she had to go on and make her life. A break of two years was mentioned.

'Well, we'll still meet from time to time,' I said, 'because we still have a terrible lot left to talk about, all sorts of world topics to discover, right?'

'Right,' she said.

Ridiculous. She phoned a couple of times. Then one day I rang her to say that Gibney was presenting a huge project in the Shelbourne to which all the major industry players were invited. I sold it well. There would be scale models and, really, any aspiring young architect should be there.

She arrived, we embraced, and it was all very decorous – until the presentation ended at half past eight and Gibney said we should have a drink. And the chemistry sparked up again.

'I believed we had a pact,' she said.

'We did and I will honour it,' I said.

Up to a point. Until one day she rang to tell me she was going to marry Larry Granville. I think I said, 'Congratulations – what's he like?'

'He's a very, very nice man, wouldn't be your type,' she replied.

Undoubtedly true on both counts. A friend described him as 'completely un-John-like', in the sense that he was a listener, the kind you'd spend a very nice evening with and realise you had told him everything and he had told you nothing.

Like me, Larry was a good deal older than Marian. He was a child in May 1941 when a Luftwaffe bomb dropped on the North Strand – the same incident that triggered our childhood flight to Granny Cosgrove's in Granard. The North Strand bomb was one of several dropped over Dublin that night and was the most catastrophic, leaving 28 dead and 90 injured, with 300 houses destroyed and hundreds homeless.

Larry's family home and livelihood were destroyed, I believe.

When they went to Rome to get married, her mother was delighted, of course, because the pope was nearby. Marian was a conflicted 24-year-old, but if there were doubts about marriage and commitment, it was Larry apparently who expressed them. I know only that Marian suggested they just go home and pretend they had got married. But whatever ensued, they got married as planned. She never talked about it, and I never asked her.

Shortly after the wedding she rang to say they were living in Ranelagh and asked if Catherine and I would like to come to dinner. Delighted, I said. It was just the four of us and a lot of drink was consumed. We were two very nervous souls, Finucane and I, as the old magic flared again.

Soon after she rang for advice about the house – she'd painted it all in psychedelic colours, I seem to remember – and I suggested lunch. After about a year of this charade, she felt conscience-bound to tell Larry that she had met me again. Not surprisingly, he considered me a very bad influence on her and offered to meet me to straighten things out.

He was admirably restrained when we met. We discussed the affair Marian and I had had – the one before she was married, specifically. I mentioned our tremendous affection for each other and said we were sticking to the rules. Larry was sceptical and expressed the view that we were a sort of poison for each other so, naturally, he drew the line at the platonic relationship I was proposing. Broadly speaking, he said it would be unwise to pursue it any further.

His entreaties failed, I'm afraid.

Our relationship continued. Our meeting point most evenings was the Shelbourne hotel. We were reminded of this some years ago when Marian and I were walking down Stephen's Green and we encountered the former concierge Jimmy Dixon, whom I hadn't seen for a long time. We all said hello, then he stopped and, in his very punctilious way, turned to Marian and said, 'I watched you falling in love. It was a wonderful thing to watch.' It was emotional. Marian started crying.

I suspect Jimmy wouldn't have been quite so enamoured of the love story had he known about the disruption left behind.

We ate a lot at Bernardo's and proceeded from there to a kip of a nightclub across the road until the early hours. Then we went home to our respective partners. As time went on, we drifted away from the party scene and Arthur Gibney would join us for lunch or dinner, three old fogeys together.

It couldn't carry on like that, obviously. We were careening towards decision time. Her marriage wasn't working, and we had to decide if we had a future together.

Meanwhile, Marian had made the jump to RTÉ, and, after a wobbly start, her career was picking up.

*

Hindsight is a wonderful thing. We know now that Marian developed whole areas of radio real estate that were previously graveyards. She opened up the afternoons with *Women Today* and *Liveline* and, between Anne Farrell and herself, created the weekends with Saturday- and Sunday-morning programmes. Shows slotted snugly around her vast audiences for groundbreaking radio, much of it rooted in her endless curiosity about what people were saying.

Her family were not to know all that, of course, when she abandoned college and a safe professional career to enter what they considered a den of iniquity. It was actually worse than they imagined. The state broadcaster that ritually lashed businesses for mistreating employees put her on a two-week contract with risible pay and conditions. That eventually rose to six months and finally, after four or five years, to a full-time contract when she was working an 80-hour week and still earning nothing close to a decent hourly wage.

Like a lot of women at that time, Marian couldn't bring herself to discuss money with RTÉ or anyone else. She would fall apart first. But she loved the job and was a natural at it, and I think she genuinely felt she would be ejected if she made any demands, however modest. She had a point. RTÉ was a monopoly, the only game in town. She was snookered.

The upside was that she happened to arrive at what was probably the most exciting era in the station's history.

Michael Littleton was there, a chess player, placing himself as the buffer between the new kids and a deeply conservative RTÉ. Littleton was a champion of public service broadcasting and a great and brave mentor to Marian and others. He made it his business to broaden the intake, seeking out different social backgrounds and authentic city and regional accents to replace the incumbents with their notions of sounding like the BBC. He gave the young bloods attitude, a chance to test themselves and try new things.

The result was a coalition of young tigers, with producers such as Patrick Farrelly and Clare Duignan, who wanted to change the world in different ways and would remain part of a tight gang. When the seniors went off on their holidays, the kids were ready to put in the hours and throw new ideas into play. When a bank holiday Monday was hit with a spate of bank robberies and the production team was discussing how to package the story, Farrelly – who had gone to school on Dublin's northside and had a broader social spectrum to call on – had the startling idea of interviewing a couple of bank robbers. He located such a pair and Marian did the interviews.

Finucane proved that she could be put in a room with anyone and take proceedings to a different level. And no one would be better prepared. She would go home and listen to the interview tapes over and over, and by the time she was back with the sound engineer, she would have it timed to the last breath. The bank robbers item caused a huge commotion, of course, particularly among the forces of law and order, but it was a symbol of things to come.

With no commercial radio competition in 1978, the audience for RTÉ radio was massive. Typically, half the country would be listening. Through producer Betty Purcell's contacts in the women's movement, Farrelly arranged a meeting with two women who worked in prostitution, Lyn Madden and Dolores Lynch (who was later murdered). These were the kind of marginalised voices that had never been heard on RTÉ before, and Marian's approach was a long way from the traditional interview. 'The best of luck to you,' she said to the two women at the end. No one had ever heard the like of that on RTÉ.

The quiet facilitator was Michael Littleton. When Finucane told him she wanted to do a programme on abortion, he gave her the go-ahead provided it was 'broadcastable', as he put it. It was a first for RTÉ and an extraordinarily brave move by Littleton. Abortion was still a criminal offence and contravened every kind of religious, social and cultural taboo.

He gave her the green light at a time when the state broadcaster was being torn apart by government influence, by the Knights of Columbanus, by the Stickies, by the communists. There were factions within factions and the Church was playing a huge role. The subject was so sensitive that even within the RTÉ newsroom people kept their views to themselves.

In truth, this was all grist to Finucane's mill. She had debated the issues from every angle. She worked 16-hour days on pure adrenaline. She researched the documentary herself and found a woman who agreed – incredibly – to be accompanied to England and to be interviewed. She sat with her throughout the abortion and the aftermath, documented it all, scripted it and spent three weeks editing it, working day and night. I suspect the entire documentary was complete before the accredited producer even got sight of it. In the end, she did as Littleton had asked: she made a broadcastable programme on abortion, a revolutionary piece of historical importance in style and substance. They called it *Abortion: The Lonely Crisis*.

This was only one of her preoccupations when we were heading for decision time in our relationships.

As the break-ups were looming, *Women Today* went on air five days a week, from two to three in the afternoon, presented by Marian and produced by Claire Duignan and Betty Purcell. It was no cosy middle-of-the-road production. *Women Today* was central to the development of the women's movement at a time when over-the-counter contraceptives were illegal and divorce was still 15 years away.

That was probably her favourite time on radio. She would ring me two or three times a day and say, 'You won't believe who we got' – and it would be some unfortunate who was going to get hammered for his very old ideas.

The whole decade had been swimming in the women's movement in a way. The newspapers' women's pages had moved on to subjects that were a long way from knitting and cooking, but the difference on RTÉ was that words like 'breast' and 'vagina' were being said out loud, on the radio.

It swiftly provoked a swarm of complaints 'about bias, bad language, immoral behaviour, [about] programmes about things likes incest, lesbianism, pornography, nudity, women's sexual problems being fired into a daytime slot at a time when its sister TV channel was still carrying *The Sunday Game* and Mass and earnest current affairs shows about mortgages', to quote John Caden, Gay Byrne's producer.

Several priests read Finucane off the altar, including one who called her a flea in the bed, which gave her great joy. It was not for the celebrity – never, ever for that – but for the clear signal that the message was cutting through.

'How does it feel?' I would ask.

'Great, we're getting there.'

When her abortion documentary won the Prix Italia – the equivalent of an Emmy or an Academy Award for radio – there was utter discombobulation among senior RTÉ figures. They were deeply unhappy and bewildered, which was hardly surprising. They had resolutely opposed the whole idea, then buried it in the Saturday-night documentary slot where, without promotion of any kind, it was guaranteed to vanish into the void.

Now those worthies on the RTÉ junket in Italy had to straighten themselves up swiftly when they heard, to their astonishment, that the big prize was coming to one of their own. For a programme about abortion. Now they were being forced to declare what a wondrously brave programme it was and how they had always believed it had to be done. As well as that, they had no idea where Finucane was.

She was finally tracked down to Malta, where she was bringing her marriage to an end. As with so much of Marian's private life, only a handful of people would ever know the circumstances. That's where she was, with her justifiably angry husband, when the call came telling her to get to Italy immediately, that she had won the Prix Italia for *The Lonely Crisis*. It was a very big deal in radio. And now this bloody woman had won it for the most taboo subject in the country.

Suddenly she was on a flight to Italy, accepting the award, the triumph and the plaudits, before returning to Malta to that painful scenario with Larry. In an odd, confused lather of guilt, sadness and triumph, she then moved out to a flat in Monkstown. I began to spend the occasional night there, while tiptoeing through a fog of disbelief.

*

I had commitments and, like Marian, a ton of guilt. Above all I was never a fan of confrontation.

I finally came clean with Catherine. I told her I was in love with Marian and wanted a different life and all the things one says during these terrible life-changing moments. Catherine didn't deserve this. She had a part-time job as a senior account executive – soon to be full-time – in the advertising industry, and my departure from the marriage and from Dublin effectively meant she was left for 10 or 11 days out of 14 with three boys on the cusp of their teenage years. Catherine had the unenviable task of getting the children to school, to homework and to some sort of level of stability in their emotional lives. A very, very difficult task which – as far as I can see – she did with skill and great input into the ordinariness of life. The highs and lows are only waypoints; children go to school, do their homework, and fight whatever teenage battles need to be fought, hats off to her. Most rows that I have experienced with my children were the very normal and natural pushback against parenting, but for long periods, she was the single mum and I have nothing but praise for her. And, as I more or less managed the next two children, I later had a keen awareness of the day-to-day slog. She coped well and with grace.

We separated in as civilised a manner as we could, and decided that whatever problems and differences we had, they should not be visited on our three boys, Jocelyn, Neal and Timothy, then aged 14, 12 and 10. We consulted a child psychologist, who advised us to sit down with them and tell them collectively that we were separating, that we would live in two different places and that we still loved them.

For the purposes of that chat, we first had dinner together with Jocelyn and Neal. It was unusual for me to be around the dinner table with them at that stage, so the boys were already on alert, and children aren't stupid. They anticipated that news was incoming about the relationship. We told them we still loved each other but could no longer live together. Jocelyn's reaction was relief because there was clarity at last. He wanted this horrible phase to end. Neal was relieved while simultaneously bursting into tears, worried about the fate of Belle the sheepdog, among other things.

We took Timothy to the Dropping Well pub the following day for the same chat.

While I moved into a new phase of my life, it was Catherine who handled the fallout.

There is much about Marian at this time that I do not know and could never know. For all our lives together, we each had areas of privacy into which the other never entered unless some information was first volunteered. There was a dividing line somewhere, and I'm not sure where that line was. We were always very careful about breaching it. Fine in theory, maybe, but in later years, on other matters, it seems to me now that it wasn't always the best strategy.

I never discussed Larry with her, and she never discussed Catherine with me. The only time I saw even a brief public reference to that part of her life was when she told RTÉ's Mike Murphy, 'Larry was a really, really, really nice guy. We really got on but just weren't a good marriage – you know yourself,' she said, shutting down that line of enquiry with instant effect.

It was a very strange period. The attraction that constantly pulled Marian and me together, and all the interests and curiosity we shared, had to be weighed against the fact that I had a wife and three young sons. I was in my mid-40s, and the waypoints ahead would have been me joining a golf club and Catherine joining a bridge club, or both. It all seemed so predictable. There had to be more to life.

The problem is that when you decide that, you are confronted with a choice. You pick a different life, a life of continued interest, and that means continued risk.

That was how both Finucane and I had lived so far. She was placed in the top three in the civil service exams, the holy grail of a permanent, pensionable job back then, turned it down to study architecture, and then took a punt on one of the most precarious careers around. As for me, I was never sure where the next buck was coming from. But we were full of curiosity about the world and how it worked. That was the path we set ourselves on.

We had married two decent, honourable people and we carried a lot of guilt about the hurt we were causing all around us. But so many things were happening at the same time – we were high with excitement and so many arrangements to be made. Ruling such matters out for discussion probably made them easier to bear.

FIVE

The Reynella Years: Paradise Found

The night before I took her to our first home together, Marian stayed in the Greville Arms Hotel in Mullingar and the boys and I went to collect her next morning. As we drove down the long avenue of Reynella House, past an honour guard of centuries-old oak trees, pheasants wandered in front of us and a pair of swans flew over towards the private lake on the lawn of the old country house. I have a vivid memory of her getting out and standing staring at the lake, enthralled.

I was staring at her.

She was visibly pregnant then and almost luminous in the morning sun. The scene around us felt like the culmination of a dream – a vision of how we could build our own paradise together, a place for children to roam on the Capability Brown-inspired landscape of uncluttered, sweeping pastures and gentle, rolling hills with stands and borders of native trees. A beautiful, rambling 200-year-old house where we could talk and sing and raise glasses into the early hours with our Dublin friends, with space enough for them to stay over and find brief respite from an Ireland that was a basket case of repression, socially and economically.

'You set this up,' she said delightedly.

The set-up had happened a couple of centuries before I laid eyes on it. The Reynell family had built Reynella House as a romantic spring and summer retreat, 'an elegant seat with fine improvements ... situated in a fine demesne, adorned with a lake and extensive plantations', according to a besotted writer in the 1800s.

It had a great octagonal hall and, on the floor above, an octagonal library of the same proportions, with six bedrooms in the wings. It lay at the centre of a marriage of that wonderful landscaping, an old cobblestone yard with stables and 200 acres for me to farm. At 45 or so, I was taking the gentlemanly route, as I imagined, to a rather nice life of running the household, farming, hunting and the odd financial coup, while Marian would be the financial engine that would bring in the modest, but vital, regular cash flow. I had sold the 4,000 acres of Mayo mountain, loaded up 300 long-legged mountainy sheep in the backs of trucks and transported them to the genteel slopes of Westmeath.

Standing by our own lake on that sunny morning in 1981, filled with energy and the promise of new life, everything seemed possible.

The economic hellscape of the 1980s and other catastrophes would have something to say about all that soon enough. In the meantime, our unique trick was to run calamity and Camelot in parallel, a kind of motif of our life together.

Marian flourished in our new life. She was 31 when we moved to Reynella and running a feminist juggernaut through the RTÉ radio schedules with *Women Today*. Rising at six every morning and tearing across bog roads at notorious speed from north Westmeath to Donnybrook in the south city was gruelling, but it was also a time to let ideas percolate, to allow the anxiety and necessary tension to build for the upcoming show to make it the best it could be. And for the next six years, the three-hour commute would seem like a decent enough compromise for the world we were building together in this amazing place.

An owl had taken up residence in the kitchen downstairs and would cough up furballs of dead mice, keeping the mouse population down, we liked to think. And we had bats. Attic windows had to be left open to dry out after heavy rain, and Marian lived in terror of bats getting stuck in her hair. The kids would wake up with bats sitting on their faces and casually throw them out.

A problem I hadn't anticipated with the mountainy Mayo sheep was their long legs and compulsion to jump walls. And in Reynella there were walls everywhere, so they were forever jumping over them, and we were forever getting phone calls to get the sheep off the road. Eventually we managed to cross-breed them with Suffolk, a lowland sheep with very short legs. It took three to four generations to stop them escaping and cluttering up the roads around Delvin.

When Sinéad was born, a few months after our arrival, we had a small gathering for the christening in Turin church a few miles away, with our good friends Nell McCafferty and Nuala O'Faolain – the godmother – along with John McCrossan from Marian's old Bolton Street debating group and his wife, Patricia, a teacher and educator.

No one was more surprised than John when Marian phoned him out of the blue and asked him to be godfather. The last the McCrossans had heard, Marian and Larry were still married, if precariously. I was an unknown quantity to them.

Marian was knocking around with a bounder living a sort of crazy life, and I suppose she knew that at some level there had to be a still point of sanity. I believe she reached into the past and picked John as the responsible one who would do what a committed humanist godparent should do should the need arise.

This would have been a significant consideration for a couple in our circumstances at the time. To many people, especially card-carrying Catholics, our living arrangements were an affront. Sinéad was still a tiny baby when Eileen Flynn, a teacher in a County Wexford convent school, was summarily sacked from her job for living 'openly' with a married man in the town where she worked. If that sounds remarkable from this distance, it's worth noting that it did not constitute unfair dismissal according to a High Court ruling.

When I first met him, Marian's brother Noel used to say, 'Whatever the pair of you are doing it must be great, but you'll never get your feet under my mother's table.' Marian had broken 'every rule in the book knocking around with a married fucker like you', he said. And he was speaking as an adoring brother. Marian often said it herself.

It was hardly surprising, then, that their mother, Maura, kept a wide berth from this black-hearted scoundrel. But when that continued for two or three years after Sinéad's arrival, I lost patience and rang her. 'Look, I know you don't approve of me, but your daughter and I are getting on terribly well. You have a grandchild now, and it would be a pity that for some sense of pride or some sense you have of me you wouldn't see her. We can agree to differ on how people live their lives' – now that was chancing it, I knew – 'but let's meet. Come to lunch and see your grandchild anyhow.' Maura arrived armed with her other daughters, Dorothy and Therese – who remain close to me to this day – and there was acceptance over time. She even grew fond of me, I like to think.

Ballydesmond also took a stand, apparently. As a modest continuity announcer, Marian had been elevated to 'television personality' down home in Limerick. Invitations to host the quiz for the big parish fundraiser arrived for several years, and all went well until word eased out that she was living with a married man. The invitations ceased.

In short, we were a walking scandal who had broken up two marriages and had an illegitimate child to prove it. Separation in those days was a sensation. Divorce didn't exist. Cohabitation was living in sin. To paraphrase Noel, we had a fatal attraction of some sort, and both of us in our own way felt a ton of guilt.

We tried to put our experience to good use. We had learned something about how bruising and pain are caused in marriage, and we believed we could avoid the obvious pitfalls that open up when the gloss fades and a real marriage begins. We might even have devised a list of things we would *not* do in a marriage. We agreed we would never argue. If a subject was getting a little hot and heavy, we would suspend proceedings and resume the following morning. If one or other party didn't want to do something, then let's not insist on doing it: let's find a third way. We did that all our lives. I recall debating and discussing things with Marian, but I don't believe we had a full-on argument in all our years. She was incredibly tolerant and agreeable – as long as you didn't cross certain of her principles or invade her privacy.

Then again, we were like two 15-year-olds who were obsessed with each other and never grew up, as our friend Patrick Farrelly put it. If something was unpleasant, we coped with it, usually by sweeping it into a corner and getting on with life. We lived on exciting highs by ignoring what might be lows.

A visitor once commented in mildly shocked tones that Marian and I were terribly polite to each other. The reason was blindingly obvious to us: we had something magical and we didn't want to break the spell. If we could tidy away the bad bits and leave them somewhere, it was wonderful. We managed to do that for a long, long time – actually, up to the moment Marian died.

Previous relationships were not allowed into the conversation because that was another time and another person. It could also have led to invidious comparisons.

Marian was probably the worst housekeeper in the history of housekeeping. I was the second worst. Disorganised, haphazard, indifferent and clueless are four more words I could add to describe the pair of us in domesticity. Now imagine if I was to arrive in to her from the farm and say, 'Jaysus, in my last marriage, my woman at least cleaned the kitchen.' I could write four responses and none of them would be printable. This had to be a clean slate.

Marian was a great cook but came from the far-too-precise school of written recipes, so very early on, I said I would do all the cooking and she would do the tidying away – at which she turned out to be appalling. We were realists and agreed we would do anything except housework. The deal was if we ever had spare money – which we never had, but if we found a bit, say – we would have somebody come in for a couple of hours a day.

That didn't always work out, of course. Nell and Nuala, who formed an integral part of the household on the weekends, contributed at different levels. The practical one among the four of us turned out to be Nell, who was great at cleaning and finding places to store plates and things. Nuala was also very neat, but she lived a highly independent life among groups. At the dining table her book would be propped here, just so, and her food would be over there, just so. I have memories of her reading, talking, eating, sipping and holding onto Sinéad simultaneously. There was a phase when she would also be smoking. So we brought in a law that Nuala could not read at the dinner table. No glancing at the book allowed – she had to close it. Nuala's ideas were too entertaining to be lost to the company.

One of those ideas, I recall, ingeniously captured her love of reading and travel. At a time when planes were being hijacked and held at gunpoint in a desert somewhere, Nuala had a plan for such an event, she told us. She would go up to the hijackers and offer to be the librarian for the siege. This would entail collecting all the books from the passengers so a) she would have plenty to read during the siege and b) people could come and borrow books from her. Having recorded the books and the borrowers' names and so on, she could then carry on reading while the hijackers went about their business.

We always looked forward to them arriving down at the weekends. Marian would have finished her week's work, and it was at the height of *Dallas*, the soap opera about a rich, highly dysfunctional Texan oil family who all seemed to live together. Nell and Nuala watched it together on Wednesday nights in Ranelagh and came away with two entirely different versions. We were watching it in Mullingar and would have another version. When they arrived on Friday nights, these combined intellectual forces analysed *Dallas* over dinner.

This was the fabric of our paradise, bound up with a working farm of sheep, cattle, horses, ducks and geese, a peacock strutting around and a magnificent double-walled old orchard – with the original apple trees – where we had turned the derelict chapel into a chicken coop, and as she grew, Sinéad would go to feed the chickens every morning with her cats ambling along beside her in that idyllic childhood.

When Jack was born in 1986 – with Jocelyn, his half-brother, and Patricia McCrossan appointed godparents – Sinéad was his big sister by five years, and she began to take him along on her trips to the yard, touring all her treasures at high speed and volume.

Woven through it all was the social life we had transplanted whole from Dublin to Reynella. We ran an open house. Guests congregated in the big old kitchen downstairs, which became the centre of the house, with the grand dining room alongside, and would drink, discuss, debate, sing, recite, tell stories and party into the night. Everyone had to perform, Nell would occasionally dance on tables, and a lot of people – not everyone, I should add – got very drunk.

It was the place to come at the weekends. Being in the back of beyond, it was not conveniently located, and people had to suffer the 90-minute train journey to Mullingar and be picked up – including my boys every second weekend – or they would drive. Either way, it was a bit of a trek, so they would stay for a couple of nights and spend the days out walking or visiting the pub or confiding in the sheep.

We built a world and modelled a kind of conversational salon in this place.

It was important to us and them at a time when the pro-life movement was at its peak and divorce was becoming a hot topic. Politicians, clerics, writers, artists, journalists and resisters, all of diverse views, talked about feminism, abortion, divorce, poverty and the woeful troubles in Northern Ireland around our long table, sometimes in sad, haunted exchanges in the lead-up to the eighth amendment to the constitution – where an outright abortion ban was nailed down in 1983 with a landslide vote – and the divorce referendum, which met a crushing defeat in 1986. It was also the stuff of Marian's radio work.

Jocelyn sat at the knees of women like Nuala, Nell and Sylvia Meehan and imbibed ideas and the realities of people's lives that hugely impacted and informed his education and growth.

For many of those who came to us, it was a respite from the pressures of city life, rough politics and resistances. It became a safe place to talk about how we could all move forward in that Ireland. I think it was a salve both emotionally and psychologically for some of our guests before resuming their Dublin lives.

A crucial element was that those who had children were able to bring them along. People like Hilary Orpen, Patsy Murphy, Mary Holland, Deirdre Purcell, Betty Purcell, Claire Duignan – women who in one way or another were thinkers and influencers in those crucial years and bore the brunt of active feminism – brought their children, and it was very deliberate on our part, that sense of openness to a new phase. Our kids were constantly turfed out of their own beds to make room for arriving adults. Their children were bundled in with ours wherever they landed.

After dinner we would hold dances for ourselves in the great hall with music at maximum volume. Sinéad adored the music from the film *Dirty Dancing* and would get into her party dress for it. My son Timothy did an impressive version of some of the movie's dances, and Nuala would dance and read simultaneously. Jocelyn would often be accompanied by various girlfriends, usually blonde and named after flowers.

Years later, a journalist described Reynella to me as a baptism of fire for someone unaccustomed to such an abundance of exuberance. At some stage he realised that everyone there was committed to all sorts of serious matters in their regular lives – it was just difficult to decipher what those matters were in the noise and chaos at times.

This was true. While there was a serious element to it, it was also chaos.

Luckily, Jocelyn, Neal and Timothy were coming from Catherine's house, where their lives were orderly and well organised during the week. Our house had all that unconstrained activity, plus a big annexe with a full-size pool table and a jukebox and a relaxed bedtime regime for the kids, provided everyone was at their station at 7 a.m. for the farm chores.

It was idyllic in many ways. The only problem was that we had no money.

*

We were spending crazy amounts on a fantastic lifestyle with a revenue stream that came nowhere near to meeting the outgoings. A major part of the projected income plan was hooked on an office block I was developing in Smithfield in the north inner city. It was about ten or fifteen years ahead of its time, if I say so myself, and would have incorporated a penthouse where Finucane and I planned to hide away from all the parties of the world.

Financially, it almost broke us. Everything went wrong.

I should probably mention the Micawber principle about living within one's means, to make us sound like earnest individuals. 'Annual income 20 pounds, annual expenditure 19 pounds 19 and six, result happiness. Annual income 20 pounds, annual expenditure 20 pounds ought and six, result misery.'

But we – well, I – preferred Micawber's other lesson, which was 'something will turn up'. We were in hock for a lot more than sixpence, relatively speaking, but it didn't stop the dance. We still took trips to Paris and Italy, having discovered the most economical way to get there was to buy cut-price last-minute seats on Lourdes pilgrimage flights with Joe Walsh Tours and journey on by train.

And, of course, alcohol remained a big contributor to the outgoings.

After breakfast we might have to go into Delvin for the shopping or whatever, and I recall heading for the pub in the company of Mary Holland – a well-known Irish journalist with a particular interest in Northern Ireland – and others for a hair of the dog from the night before.

'I've never had a drink at a quarter to ten in the morning,' said Mary.

'I thought you led quite a wild, unreasonable life,' I said.

'Not at a quarter to ten – what could you drink at a quarter to ten in the morning?' she wondered. To be civil, she opted for a glass of stout, which she probably left behind her. What seemed odd to Mary was a regular affair in our bailiwick.

There were other expensive habits for people with no income stream. I was hunting three days a week and kept a few racehorses – 'an adequate number', I used to say to Marian when she nervously asked for details. It wasn't so much the horses that used up the money, I realised later. It was what one could have been doing if one hadn't been drinking so much and acting the eejit. I remember telling Mary Holland that we were going to have to sell the place in the next year or two, and we were therefore obliged to curtail our living costs.

'Well, I hadn't noticed,' she said rather tartly.

The main problem was the Smithfield project, still sitting in a legal quagmire after several years, and a debt with interest rates at 22 per cent. The farm just about washed its face financially, and Marian was still earning a figurative two and fourpence a week. We were staring at disaster. A cash stream was urgently required. Rather than waiting for something to turn up, we needed to use some imagination.

Our lake had held the Irish carp record for years, so we decided to open as a guesthouse for fishermen. Fawlty Towers mark two. I loved it. Marian hated every moment of it, but she liked the North of England fishermen because all they wanted to do was fish. They fished through the night and ate a full breakfast in the morning, after which they went to bed. Then they got up around lunchtime, went into Delvin for a few pints, came back and fished. I cooked them the plain food they liked for dinner.

Our two assistants in this enterprise, when we were very busy or absent, were Nell and Nuala. Neither party could cook.

At one stage I read that Mrs Gandhi had fallen out with Mrs Thatcher and suggested to Marian that Mrs Gandhi might agree to an interview with an Irish journalist. RTÉ agreed and we headed off to India with Clare Duignan, where Marian did the interview. It was a genuine coup for the team, with the unhappy postscript that Mrs Gandhi was assassinated three months later.

Meanwhile, Nell and Nuala had arrived down to take charge of Sinéad and run hospitality for four pre-booked English fishermen. 'How is it going?' we asked when we finally got through on the phone from Delhi.

'Those chickens are terribly hard,' said Nell. 'We're having trouble roasting them for the guests.'

'You have to defrost them, Nell, and *then* you roast them …'

When the hard chickens wouldn't roast for them the first night, they decided they would give the fishermen gin and tonics to delay the dinner. Then the staff decided they needed some gin and tonics to soothe themselves. Finally, they sent down to Delvin for fish and chips. They sank two bottles of gin between the six of them. A wonderful time was had by all.

We weren't keen on American guests because they were very fussy and wanted four-star service and accommodation for B&B prices. I think our rate was £10. We generally turned them away, but a family arrived one day from West Virginia, helped around the farm, stayed for a week and loved it all. The following year we were baffled when Americans started arriving in droves. We only figured out why when we discovered that the West Virginians had written us up in Fodor's tourist guide as the best guesthouse to stay in Ireland. While the staff were running the show in our absence, it must have been a walking disaster for the guests. Nuala was writing her column for the *Irish Times* and Nell was getting on with hers. But the worse it got, the more the Americans seemed to like it.

All this meant we were able to put groceries on the table but nothing more. We were bleeding money.

However, sometimes things did turn up, as Micawber decreed.

One night Marian and I went to a fundraiser in the Hirschfeld Centre – a safe social hub for gay people at a time when homosexual acts were still criminalised – and a man came over to enquire about the guesthouse. He was organising a weekend for about a hundred people who would bring their own tents. 'Delighted to do it,' I said, offering to provide the catering as well with all the unwarranted confidence of someone who had never cooked for more than 10.

The Hirschfeld trip was a sensitive matter for everyone involved, and we had concerns about it leaking to the media. So, I approached the head chef of a large facility for advice about cooking for numbers and told him it was a boy scout leaders' group coming for a jamboree. We thought it best to confine the jamboree to the farmland, so we bought a thousand pounds' worth of beer and wine off the local publican, which kept him happy. The chef agreed to work for three days for us for a fee. Nell and Nuala were appointed as chief waitresses, along with Clare Duignan. Jocelyn became the washer-upper with a few others.

Come the appointed weekend, the chef turned up with a massive electric pot into which he threw 60 chickens and all manner of things. The 'boy scouts' arrived en masse with their tents and lit a huge campfire by the lake and sang 'My Bonnie Lies over the Ocean'. It was a roaring success. I remember standing having a smoke with the chef, watching the dancing, when two of the men exchanged a kiss. The cigarette suddenly dropped from his fingers as the truth dawned, but he made a rapid recovery.

The only problem for accounting purposes was that our guests were an exceptionally healthy lot and hardly drank a can of beer between them, so the staff were pleased to help drink some of the thousand pounds of liquor. Most of the guests didn't smoke either, while the smoke clouds puffing out of the kitchen windows were blinding.

The following Monday I went down to Delvin for my cure, where I met Paddy Shaughnessy, the bar owner and supplier of all the liquor.

'Some of the boy scouts were in here yesterday,' he said. 'They're very nice lads. Did you do all right out of them?'

'We did very well – they had a great time,' I said.

'I'll tell you what,' said Paddy, 'maybe next year you'll get the girl guides.' Upon which I maintained an unusual silence.

Another windfall that buoyed our finances in a serious way in 1984 was an RTÉ/Channel 4 movie, *Summer Lightning*, adapted from a Turgenev novel and translated to pre-famine Ireland by Derek Mahon and Paul Joyce. Joyce was also directing a pretty impressive cast that included Paul Scofield, Donal McCann, Dearbhla Molloy, Maureen Toal and Tom Bell. We were an excellent choice as a location. They were able to use the house, the lands and the cobblestone yard – which was turned into a village – and that worked very well for us because we got the rental for each. The kids got work as extras, and as we also provided the catering, they worked long days as kitchen runners so got decent chunks of money in the deal.

*

None of this was solving the long-term problem for us, however. And bizarre things seemed to befall us. One afternoon out of the blue, Brian McNicholl, our former builder from the Smithfield debacle, arrived at the house with a female companion. 'Will we go for a drink?' I said – hello, of course we'll go for a drink – and he drove me and Sinéad to O'Shaughnessy's pub in Delvin.

Quite a lot of drink was being consumed amid joy and bonhomie, and McNicholl was buying it, which was very unusual.

Marian arrived to collect Sinéad and me and we drove home. About an hour later McNicholl arrived at the door and asked if he could stay the night – it was a guesthouse, after all. No, said Ms Finucane crisply, there were people expected. That was unlike her. There may well have been other people around, but Marian had different reasons for the sharp refusal. McNicholl's previous life as a security guard had come back to bite him. She recognised him from the Hume Street site, where there had been intimations of some rough handling.

He stayed in a guesthouse in Delvin that night, and I remember mentioning to Marian that he was carrying a big wad of cash and suggesting that something was afoot. The next morning Marian left for work at six; Sinéad and I were chewing the fat when he reappeared with his friend, only this time he looked like a different man – frightened, anxious, white-faced and without a trace of yesterday's bonhomie.

'I need to talk to you. I'm in a spot of bother,' he said.

'What's the trouble?' I asked.

'I was involved in the kidnap of Jennifer Guinness,' he said. 'In a minor way, you understand.'

The kidnapping of Jennifer Guinness by an armed gang for a two-million-pound ransom had been leading every news bulletin for the past eight days.

Life is full of bizarre coincidences and here was another one. Jennifer Guinness was married to John Guinness, whose brother was married to my first cousin. And like the whole of Ireland, we had followed every detail of the kidnapping. So, a sort-of-in-law is kidnapped and this comedian has just told me he's involved.

'Where is she?' I asked.

'I think they found her,' he said.

Now this was hot news unknown to the country at large. 'But where is she?'

She was in his female friend's flat in Waterloo Road.

So the reason he was driving around and looking for discreet lodgings was because his friend and McNicholl himself couldn't go home.

I think I said, 'Get the hell of out here – I don't want the police around us.'

I took the bus with Sinéad to Dublin that afternoon, and Marian was picking us up at Busáras, as arranged. She was parked outside, glued to the radio, and instead of the usual greeting said, 'Shh, they've found Mrs Guinness.'

'Marian,' I said carefully, 'You might not believe this … Mrs Guinness was found in an apartment on Waterloo Road and McNicholl was in on it.' Marian's mouth fell comically open – as it always did when she heard interesting news. 'What are we going to do?' I asked.

Finucane was well ahead of me. 'We're going straight to the police. Tonight,' she said, when I balked a bit. There was no turning the woman in this mode. 'You have a responsibility to society and you have to tell the truth.'

Marian was always my moral wall. She would say about certain dilemmas, 'No, that's wrong, that shouldn't be. I don't like you doing things like that.' She was the bulwark.

So very soon I was talking to a slightly incredulous senior garda in Drumcondra police station, who was looking for timelines.

McNicholl gave himself up that day. And whatever else was going on, our house suddenly had an invasion of undercover detectives that evening who suspected a gang member was in the area, I gathered. I was under armed guard for several weeks for reasons never fully explained.

McNicholl was brought up on kidnapping and firearms charges, but by the time the trial started, several witnesses suddenly found they had other urgent business to attend to. That left me virtually alone as a witness. Marian came to court for the three days I was on the stand, and I have a feeling she quite enjoyed it. McNicholl's defence counsel put the boot in, questioning my memory – as he was entitled to do: 'So you were with your daughter and she was four, and you were drinking in a pub all day long ...?' True, I'm afraid. Although he played a fairly minor role and I encouraged him to confess, McNicholl denied everything, for reasons best known to himself. He got 12 years.

*

This was all quite diverting, but by now we had run out of financial options in Reynella House. Nothing was turning up and selling up was inevitable. And for all her powerful energy and determination, Marian was tiring of the daily three-hour commute and the tailbacks. At the beginning, no one had believed she would keep it up, and, Finucane being Finucane, she set out to prove them wrong.

Meanwhile she was moving into uncharted territory for RTÉ. With *Liveline* she and Hilary Orpen had started the first dedicated phone-in show, the first to rely completely on callers picking up the phone. And from what I remember, in the early weeks of its life there was a terrible problem. People wouldn't ring them – probably because they felt it was above their station to speak out, and who would listen to them, and what would others think of them? It certainly played a role in the cracks that were appearing in society. Listen to the callers to Joe Duffy today: his phone lines could be blocked for the next thousand years – everybody has a point of view.

Meanwhile, the commute was taking its toll on Finucane. She was taking a grim pride in making it into RTÉ through a wall of snow when people living 10 miles out couldn't hack through it. It took five hours in the jeep one day. So with or without the financial problems, it was obvious our days in Reynella House were numbered.

I was always philosophical about the twists and turns of life. Sometimes you go up and sometimes you go down. I never went for proper, permanent jobs or pensions or security. Life sort of happened. I've lived in about twenty houses over my lifespan. A house is a house, even Reynella, where I remember nothing but the good times and the fun we had. It had to end sometime.

We drew a circle within a 30-mile radius of Dublin and found a house and a small farm in Kilteel, County Kildare – the back of beyond in those days but half the journey time to Donnybrook. Nuala gave us a short-term loan of ten thousand quid, and we bought the Georgian house and 40 acres for £48,000. Some might recognise it as Flurry Knox's residence in *The Irish RM*, the 1980s TV series based on the Somerville and Ross stories. It was cheap for a reason. In true Hollywood tradition, it was no more than a façade. The interior had long since rotted away and the place was a shell.

I had quite a job ahead to make it habitable.

SIX

Sinéad: Too Busy to Cry

I have a vivid memory of Sinéad at about four, squatting intently over a box and busily tearing the paper off it, when a wasp stung her on the bottom. There was a loud yelp.

Marian started laughing. 'Does it not hurt?'

'I'm just too busy to cry at the moment,' said Sinéad.

It was almost a metaphor for Finucane the mammy. When we were planning our last trip to India, the state of Marian's heart and health was a contentious subject. 'You're really sick – you must go back to the doctor,' I said over and over. It was a constant theme but was always going nowhere. She knew she was very unwell. But there was unfinished business and fun in India.

If Sinéad was just too busy to cry, Marian was just too busy to die.

They were two peas in a pod.

While the house was being made habitable, very slowly, we moved to a place on Haddington Road and jogged along in our own incompetent way. It took me a year to do up the house in Kilteel.

We were battling our way out of the 1980s depression, getting big chunks of debt off our backs, climbing slowly out of a financial swamp. 'Why are we always bloody skint?' Marian used to say – but the tide was turning. We had overcome the Smithfield disaster, Marian's *Liveline* ratings were soaring, and she won Radio Journalist of the Year. Century Radio, God bless it (as we always referred to it), had upended the broadcasting market for presenters. A shift in fortunes was on the cards.

*

We were living on Haddington Road when Sinéad made her First Holy Communion in the local church.

The convent school catered for a broad cross-section of children, but Marian always felt the nuns were cold relics of Archbishop McQuaid. Her mother's story of McQuaid's insult to the illegitimate child at the Confirmation had never stopped spinning somewhere in her head.

Marian was quintessentially polite – she just couldn't be otherwise. She would cross countries to avoid confrontation. But she had a row with the nuns. There were twins, a boy and a girl, friends of Sinéad's who lived down the road, and the nuns wouldn't let them make their First Holy Communion together. The rule was that the boys had to be on one side and the girls on the other. It might have seemed like a strange hill to die on, but it was precisely the old 1950s religious mindset that drove Marian's anger. She had words with the reverend mother but failed to change her mind.

We had a party after the ceremony in the garden of the house, and on Sinéad's instructions all the women had to wear hats. Photographs from the day show her and Jack wearing the same hats as the ladies, and Nell is wearing two. It was an inflection point in our lives, in more ways than one.

Soon after, we moved into a barely finished Kilteel. We were driving home from Mayo one day, and I have a vivid memory of Sinéad perched, as always, just behind us between the two front seats, chattering away. Somewhere amid the chirpy torrent, she mentioned a terrible pain in her leg. Largely unconcerned, we took her to the GP anyway – and suddenly the world as we knew it began to spin away from us.

Then we were in Harcourt Street Children's Hospital, sitting across from three doctors and a nurse and, ominously, a woman who introduced herself as a counsellor. We, who had lived a life of joy and fun, had swept problems into corners, avoided confrontation at all costs and swerved clear of calamity countless times, had landed in the kind of trouble from which we could not avert our eyes.

We probably came across as a strange pair. I believe we may have been quite breezy – 'Hello, how are you, is there a problem?'

'Your daughter has myeloid lymphoblastic leukaemia.'

'What?' We must have looked mystified or bewildered.

'It's a fatal disease.' There was a 3 to 5 per cent chance of survival. Dazed silence.

Marian started crying. I reverted to my customary what-is-it-just-fix-it mindset. They explained what it was, what they thought might happen and how they might cure it. The general consensus was it was going to be very, very hard. But they had a plan. The man in charge was Professor Temperley from Trinity, a very nice man whom I got to know very well.

We left the hospital, crossed the road to the Harcourt Hotel, ordered two whiskeys, sat down and looked at each other and asked the question: 'How will we cope?' We had only a hint of what lay ahead – a year of paralysing fear and despair, hope and euphoria, before plunging back into despair. On repeat. A trial of every family sinew, nerve and relationship stretched and tested to breaking point. And for Marian and me, one that would culminate in a dilemma that only happens in nightmares.

Sinéad was running happily around the place when we got home. 'We'll bring her in next week,' I said to a doctor on the phone.

'No, bring her in tomorrow,' he said.

'Why?'

'Because it's in the bone marrow and children's bone marrow changes with alarming rapidity.'

My next instinct after the just-fix-it phase was to seek out second opinions, just in case Irish medicine was lagging behind the world. We had a connection with a professor of biochemistry in the University of Chicago who was very involved in cell research, and the plan was to send one sample to him and another to the Mayo Clinic. The next challenge for us was to get them to both destinations within 12 hours of the blood extraction. With a lot of cooperation and coordination, Neal got them there on time, partly by having a car waiting on the tarmac in New York to speed him to another waiting plane for Chicago.

The laboratory analysis confirmed what we already knew. The Irish doctors had missed nothing.

We knew now that our options were very limited.

The urgent next step was to start chemotherapy. A three-month treatment plan was drawn up. There was great uncertainty then about chemotherapy regimens for children. Research was slight and a small misjudgement could kill.

The treatment meant that Sinéad would have to live in the hospital for three months. I remember Marian and me bringing her in, each of us terrified, to a ward with six or eight kids in it, every one of them bald. I could feel Marian shrinking beside me.

'I don't think I'll be able to cope with this,' she said when we left Sinéad to settle in.

'We don't have choices,' I said. We talked at length.

'Would you mind if I work through this?' she asked. 'I have to keep working. I can't sit around and wonder and wait – and you're better with cuts and bruises.'

'Today?'

'Yes,' she said.

'Of course I wouldn't mind,' I said.

It was around this time that we employed Kathleen Lambe, from Kilteel village, to take care of Jack, who was just three years old. Over the years, Kathleen became enmeshed in family life as our days were swallowed up by hospital appointments, terrifying procedures, treatment schedules, rosters and the ongoing need to make a living and make the house habitable while maintaining some level of normality around the small boy.

As that autumn shaded into winter, Marian went into work every day to do the afternoon programme. Work was her saviour. Her Valium, as she described it, was the long early-morning walks across the Kildare hills with Nuala O'Faolain. I feel they talked about things that women only confide in each other, and it might be what saved her sanity. Her astonishing ability to show up at work every day and sound normal on a live show was a tribute to the brilliant, loyal team around her who carried her through those months.

I was in the hospital most afternoons and she would arrive in at around four or five, and we would stay with Sinéad till around six or seven, when other people started coming in. The terrible rollercoaster of Sinéad's changing condition determined whether we went home or across the road for a few drinks. The discussion rarely veered beyond Sinéad – was she up today or was she down, what could we do, who could we talk to ...

In the hospital ward, some incidents are branded in my brain. The chemotherapy infusions came in a silver bag, and one morning a bag split as the nurse was carrying it to a bedside. I stood watching, stunned, as the liquid splashed on the floor and began to burn through the linoleum. While staff tried to scrub it away, I could only think – that toxin is being fed into our child.

I remember the children's terror of the lumbar punctures and the terrible silence on the ward that preceded them. All I could do was hold Sinéad's hand and promise a McDonald's and Coke next day.

On the day after one such lumbar puncture, Neal had just arrived home from America and Timothy was with him. Sinéad had lost her hair and a wig carefully chosen by Marian had vanished – probably decorating a lamb in Kilteel. I declared it a celebration day and said we were going for lunch.

'Is the lumbar puncture bad?' Neal asked her chattily as we drove around Stephen's Green towards McDonald's.

'It means two Cokes and a Big Mac,' she said cheerfully. She was a get-on-with-it-get-over-it kind of girl. To her, everything about life was fascinating and there was always an upside. Too busy to cry.

Jocelyn was in college and spent most of his evenings sitting with Sinéad, reading stories and talking.

What we learned from Harcourt Street hospital was that they found it easier to talk to the children about their illness than the adults, and so the children were given all the information. In Harcourt Street, the nurses talked to them at length, named their illness, explained what they were doing with different treatments and how they were going to do it. They treated the children as adults and the adults as children, and that made sense to us. The kids were totally familiar with all the procedures and their purpose. Sinéad knew exactly what she had. 'I have myeloid leukaemia,' she would say to anyone who enquired.

One day the young final-year doctors were in for their exams and were directed to talk to particular children, identify what was wrong with them, what the procedure should be and write their reports. I recall the matron standing there, observing that some doctors were very slow. 'Every child in there,' she said, 'if you ask them what's wrong, they'll give you the brief, the breakdown, the medication – because they have been told.' All the doctors had to do was ask them. They would have told them every detail, right down to what happened in theatre.

We looked for ways to distract them. Another little boy and girl in the ward also had leukaemia, and I decided to cheer up the three of them by asking friends around the world to send them postcards from famous people, supposedly. The campaign was a big success. One day, all three of them got a card from the queen in Buckingham Palace – well, it certainly had an English stamp and a picture of the palace; the next might be a few lines from an Egyptian prince; and the next from the American president in the White House. My friends performed brilliantly from their various locations around the world and the looks on the children's faces as each card arrived gave us all incredible joy.

Sinéad was acutely conscious of her mortality. 'Am I going to die?' she asked Jocelyn one evening. The question would probably have floored me. It can't have been easy for him, but he felt they needed to be truthful with each other.

'We don't know, but we hope not,' he said, 'and this treatment is one way of dealing with it.'

Whatever you did, you didn't lie to them. The reality of her life was confronting her every day as she watched other children die. In a ward with six or eight children, we never knew from day to day who would be alive or dead. They all had basins; they would all talk to you, then almost casually turn and puke in the basin. These were all children who were living with death and dying in a very intimate and real way.

Some of them survived, went home with happy parents

and never spoke of it because they retained no memory of it. Others died.

Sinéad seemed soothed by Jocelyn's answer. It wasn't the only time she asked that question.

He loved being there in those night-time hours. He would sit and read while she slept or introduced other kids to him. She fell in love with a boy who had no hair. The boy survived and left – and forgot about her. The girl beside her died, and sometimes when friends died, she turned angrily away from visitors, refusing to speak. Yet what I remember more than anything is the sound of laughter, the loud chatter, the fun of racing each other on trollies, the nurses who let children be children.

And I remember when we realised that the treatment, horrific as it was, was failing.

A bone marrow transplant became our only hope.

The procedure was at a very early stage of its development and carried risks of multiple complications, but we were out of options. All of Sinéad's siblings, as well as Marian and I, were tested for donor compatibility. Bizarrely, I was the only one that was a near match.

To be a healthy donor, I had to stop drinking for a month beforehand, which was fair enough. The procedure itself, by which they drill into your bone to harvest the living marrow, was unexpectedly painful. I've described the aftermath as a sore bottom; it was a pain deep in the bone, which induced some limping around for a while.

But the truly extraordinary part of it all was the outcome. It worked. While Sinéad was confined in a kind of sterile bubble for a couple of months and limited to a few visitors, she grew visibly healthier. Her hair started to grow again. The odds for her recovery soared. It was breathtaking to watch. By March, she was in remission and allowed to go home. We began to rediscover how normality felt and even to consider the future again.

It was the summer of Italia '90, and Ireland was wild with excitement about the Irish soccer team's progress. Nell and Nuala were coming back and forth, and we used to go up to the Kilteel Inn with the kids to watch the matches. The sun seemed to shine a lot.

Then Sinéad mentioned a pain. We knew immediately what it meant. We drove her straight to Harcourt Street. By the time we got home, we had word that the leukaemia had reappeared in another form. There was an infection – perhaps in the permanent cannula above her chest, we were told. And that infection had possibly triggered an immune response that reignited the leukaemia that was now metastasising across her body.

Whatever the cause, the disease took such a rare form at that point, in that it was morphing from one type of leukaemia to another and back, that the specialist Swiss databank had only the most minimal information on it. The doctors were attempting to treat a moving target.

This time we knew there was no coming back.

*

What now? We met with the doctors. They were dogged, planning to start again. We asked them to be as truthful as possible with us. What were our chances? They said 5 to 10 per cent. Were they fairly confident about that? More like 1 to 2 per cent, maybe.

I kept asking questions, even in the hopelessness.

'We're coping with it,' Professor Temperley said, 'but we really don't know it.'

'Well, your team is not as philosophical as you are,' I said.

'We train them to be terriers, to never give up,' he replied.

For seemingly endless, torturous days Marian and I talked about what we should do next. Would we go again with a second treatment? Would we put the child through this unremitting torture again – for what? In the end, we reached the only rational decision: that she shouldn't suffer any more.

I was dispatched to see Professor Temperley to tell him we had decided to stop treatment, to say we just wanted Sinéad home with us to enjoy whatever time she had left. We were unusual in that, apparently, but at those percentages we were not going to torture this child any more.

The doctors were adamant that she should stay in hospital for the best kind of care, a not-so-subtle code, we realised, for pain management and horribly unpredictable episodes towards the end. We were equally adamant that we wanted her home, that Sinéad would want to be home and we would have help to cope.

'How long have we got?' I asked.

'Nine to ten weeks,' Professor Temperley said.

We met other unlucky parents in the same terrible predicament who made a different call. 'You don't think about regrets,' Marian said. 'You make a call and, either way, you have to believe this is the right one for our child.' We heard all the stories of miracle cures, the ones about a child who was on the point of death and suddenly recovered. They featured in our waking nightmares. Who are we? Do we have the right to do this? We are the parents, yes, but who ultimately is making the decision? Us? The doctors? God?

We made the call.

Nine to ten weeks.

How do you fill that short and precious time in a way that matters? With joy, we decided.

We asked her what she would like to do. Sinéad being Sinéad, she was way ahead of us, producing what would now be called a bucket list.

She wanted to be a barman. That was on the list.

'I have a new employee for you,' I said to John Brennan in the Kilteel Inn.

'Well, she can pull pints but only for an hour a day,' he said.

So she pulled pints, while the mammy and daddy sat and drank, and everyone who came in heroically insisted that their pint be pulled by Sinéad.

She wanted to learn to ride a horse. Right, we said, and went down to the local stables, where she learned to ride a pony – or thought she did, which was all that mattered.

And she wanted a dog. Forget all the rules of the house about no dogs upstairs and all that. Rex, a lurcher of some dodgy parentage, came upstairs and slept on her bed. He was quite a difficult dog, but she loved him and he loved her.

The boys made her an integral part of their daily lives, chatting to her and reading stories. Nuala bought her the most appalling, gaudy jewels and dresses and Sinéad loved them all. Everyone watched out for Jack and maintained the solid base that kept us going.

A kind of tradition had developed where Sinéad went on her annual holidays for a few days to the McCrossans, who live near the Phoenix Park in Dublin. As time went on, Jack joined her for a few days filled with treats and outings. We wanted nothing to seem out of the ordinary, so we maintained that tradition to the end.

There is a remarkable photograph of Sinéad and Jack taken in those days. They've spotted a playground in a hollow near the People's Park and raced down the embankment helter-skelter. All Sinéad's dark hair has grown back, her face is glowing, and her eyes are sparkling with life. She had four weeks to live.

Back home, even then, the house was full of kids running around, with Sinéad leading the pack.

There is an inevitability about dying for older people which makes it more tolerable, I think. To sit looking at a nine-year-old who is your own creation, to listen to her singing and to laugh at her jokes and tricks while considering where you will bury her in a few weeks, is a unique form of torture.

We had to find a grave for our child. The obvious place

was the new cemetery in Eadestown, but Marian wanted her to be nearer to us. I think she had her heart set on the old cemetery that lay between us and the village, set in an undulating pastoral landscape among the ruins of a monastic settlement and an eighth-century church, purportedly linked to the Knights Templar. It had been closed for years.

By a benign twist of fortune communicated by Kathleen, it emerged that all the family of her mother, Mammy Lambe, were buried there. A practical woman, Mammy Lambe wanted to be buried with her husband in Eadestown and saw no reason why Sinéad could not be accommodated in an old Lambe plot. Even without the help of headstones, Joe O'Neill, a local man, was able to identify one that had room for two. The Lambes' generosity meant not only a resting place in this extraordinary location for Sinéad – but ultimately a place next to her for Marian.

I put in a therapeutic few hours cutting back the overgrowth.

Four weeks. Three weeks ... We were measuring her decline like a slow hourglass running out.

All of Kilteel was waiting with us. People were calling, bringing gifts, not knowing what to say but showering us with kindness.

We talked endlessly to palliative-care people and to the hospice. How do you cope? What do you do?

Some details remained seared in our souls.

'The first thing to do is get rid of all your white towels,' said the nurse, a very pleasant, kind woman. Near the point of death, we were warned, there was a risk of dramatic haemorrhage, and heavy bleeding on white towels would terrify the child. 'So get towels in deep blues and greys and deep reds,' she advised.

We had row upon row of pharmaceuticals on shelves, some of which went into a painkiller cocktail and, as the pain worsened, were delivered via a syringe pump. We had to focus hard to grasp the sequence of those injections. They were on a tray in the kitchen with the various hypodermics, and every night we practised a particular procedure, just in case.

As time grew short, we moved a little bed into our room so that she was beside us and someone was always with her as she faded gently away from us.

Near the end, we brought her down to the sitting room, and Marian lay on a daybed with her child cradled over her heart. Rex the dog was in and out and everyone took time to sit with her. She was almost comatose by then, though she briefly woke to ask Jocelyn if she was going to die, and he said yes. 'I'm not afraid,' she said. Nell and Nuala made dinner. Marian was persuaded to take a break for a few minutes while I held Sinéad. And with that, our child took her last breath in my arms.

Professor Temperley's prediction was just a week out.

Neal carried her up the long, wide stairway to her bedroom and laid her on her bed, and family, friends and neighbours kept vigil through the night.

As we said a last goodbye before she was placed in the coffin, people lined the stairs all the way to her room. There was the sound of muffled weeping and men removed their caps as the little coffin was borne downstairs and placed in our Vauxhall estate for Sinéad's last drive to the village. She was ours. She would not be going in a hearse with strangers.

Inside the church, Jack ran up to the coffin and started banging one of the handles like a door knocker. 'Sinéad! Sinéad! Are you in there? Can you hear me?'

Marian's cousin, Monsignor Ciaran O'Carroll, then the rector in the Irish College in Rome and now the parish priest in Donnybrook, said the funeral Mass, and Kathleen sang 'Ag Críost an Síol' at Marian's request.

At the end, Neal, Jocelyn, Tadhg Hassett – Therese's husband – and I carried Sinéad's coffin out to the car and drove down the road to the old graveyard. Like creatures from another era, we carried her from the roadside across the grassy field past the cattle and the ancient ruins, through the gate in the old stone wall to her resting place.

'What happens to Sinéad now?' asked Jack, as he, the boys and a friend's seven-year-old were being driven to the reception.

'Jack, it's so exciting,' said the little girl breathlessly. 'Sinéad gets into a lift and the lift goes all the way up and then it goes *ping* ... and it opens, and she steps out and everywhere she looks there are mountains and mountains of sweets and all these other children and they're all playing and running ...' As she listed all the sweets, the boys saw a notable shift in Jack. From the anger, confusion and frustration we had witnessed the night before, he seemed to settle. He knew where his sister was now, and it sounded pretty good. Thank God for Joanne O'Sullivan, that seven-year-old girl, and all the little girls like her.

Kathleen spun another story for him that Sinéad was going to heaven in a magic box and that she would have the special job of turning on the stars at night. He also saw the point of that.

Eventually the crowds abated, the house emptied out, and Marian and I settled up to one another, whiskeys in hand. I don't remember many words being exchanged.

I tried to rationalise it, as is my wont. *That's life. That's the way it is.* I thought perhaps if you carried a child you would have a more emotional attachment to that child than the father. And as might be obvious from that statement, it's also true to say that I wasn't much in touch with my emotions back then.

For Marian, the subject was simply taboo. She and I talked about Sinéad in the kind of shorthand that couples have. If someone she knew mentioned Sinéad, she just cried. If it was someone she didn't know, her eyes filled with tears and she walked away. She had no answer to her grief. When somebody suggested counselling, the response was an icy look that would stop a bus. Whatever she felt, whatever she thought, I think she took a decision that this was hers and hers alone. In a phrase that she would probably kill me for using, it was her cross to carry, something too visceral, too private to be shared with others. I believe she felt that talking about it might somehow relieve her of some connection with Sinéad that she desperately needed to keep. I think I understand that. People who suggested counselling, saying the therapist 'would help get rid of the grief', made her so angry. 'Why would I want to get rid of it?' she would say.

This was ours. Hers.

And remained like that to the day she died.

Of course, she would return over and over to all the possible causes, torturing herself for any clue at all, however unlikely, as to why this should have happened, why our wonderful daughter should die. You hang on to anything that might explain the inexplicable.

Chernobyl was raised, as it often was back then in similar contexts and illness clusters. The nuclear power plant blew up in 1986 around a time when we used to have Sinéad down on Sandymount beach, swimming, while the winds were blowing this way.

I arranged a meeting for us with Professor Temperley about six months after we lost Sinéad in the hope that it would allay Marian's terrible burden of grief. He seemed so guarded that I had to assure him that this conversation was simple curiosity, that the child was dead and we had accepted that. We just wanted to know what went wrong – if, indeed, anything had.

They didn't know enough, he said with patent honesty; they had done everything they possibly could, but he had no answers. We were probably looking back to the dinosaur era and some flawed gene tens of thousands of years ago, he said.

There was no more to be said. It did nothing to soothe

Marian's grief, but then nothing on earth was going to do that.

*

The cruel reality was that Sinéad so nearly made it. As the first child to survive a bone marrow transplant, she entered the medical literature, as did the rarity of the perfect storm that crushed her body in the end. Our child was one of those fallen soldiers whose sacrifices help to move an army further on in the battlefield. So her death, you might say, was not in vain.

Marian and Gay Byrne were not fond of each other, but they met in a corridor in RTÉ one day and he stopped and said, 'I won't ask you – I can see it in your eyes.' I feel that was the right thing, maybe the only thing, to say. People feel compelled to say something, but what is there to be said that's meaningful? Marian felt it was a rare connection between them.

She and I coped in our own way.

Marian was getting through the day in a cloud of pain but, astonishingly, still functioning in her job. She would talk about programmes and ideas, the weather, scandal, who was doing what and with whom – but there was one subject that remained taboo. Sinéad. And over the years, I honoured that silence.

She laid it down into her store of private grief that got taken out on occasion, was stirred around and put back in. We label them experiences, but they're much more profound than that. It's another level of understanding of the terrible consequences of being human.

When she couldn't find the words and the pain appeared to be crushing her, all I could do was be there for her, to cook the food and keep the wheels of domesticity turning insofar as I was able.

We would sit at home and we'd talk – what'll we do and how will we do it – usually armed with a glass of whiskey. Whatever way she was coping or not coping, it was her way and mine.

But if it sounds unrelentingly grim, I don't remember it like that.

We always went to bed together and kissed each other goodnight.

Even through the worst of times, we maintained that old trick we had of navigating two parallel lives: the life we shared together of great love and common interests, voracious reading, news monitoring, endless chat about programme ideas and the vast, wider world – and the other life of the near impenetrable, private, independent kingdoms of our inner selves.

And we managed it quite successfully, apparently. In the 10 years after Sinéad's death, we travelled widely and entertained. We even got married.

SEVEN

After Sinéad – Travels

Memories of life after Sinéad flash past through a prism of anxiety and non-stop movement, dimly discerned now through a blizzard of passport stamps, well-filled glasses, unreliable memory and, oddly, a lot of anarchic fun.

The local GP had to deliver a few gentle warnings to Marian that she might be overprotecting Jack. The impulse to have every sniffle, every pain, every bruise checked out was a natural response to catastrophe but needed a rebalance.

Nuala O'Faolain was Marian's anchor. They walked for miles around the local roads in the early mornings, giving Marian the space and time to talk out her grief. I drank and communed with Nell. And John and Patricia McCrossan turned up regularly. We had small dinner parties, for which I cooked, and we had our regular drinks party the Sunday before Christmas.

And then we started to travel. Some might sense a kind of compulsion in all the travel, a frantic need to remove ourselves from the site of great pain coupled with an urge to explore some of my wilder theories – which bereaved people will tell you only works up to a point. But whatever the motivation behind it, at least we had the cash flow now to sustain it.

Just around the time Sinéad became ill, Century Radio had come along and created a market for RTÉ stars, leverage that could be used to extract better terms from RTÉ. Marian was in demand to do all sorts of programmes. If the breadth and quality of her work appeared seamless to outsiders during that terrible period, it was because she had a brilliant team in whom she could confide and who carried her through.

She had become a darling of the press – a role she never sought or liked, given her obsession with privacy. She believed that if somebody puts you on a pedestal, the only thing you can do is fall. She also felt strongly that being a broadcaster was just a job like any other, but there was always a shortage of celebrities in Ireland, and quite often broadcasters were used to fill the vacuum. So it was 'Marian takes a swipe at this', 'Marian leads the pack', 'Marian was wearing' …

People approached her to praise or berate her wherever

she went. But she was unfailingly polite. I remember about six months into Sinéad's treatment, Marian was having a drink in the pub with a friend when a stranger, after a few drinks too many, came over to say what he thought of her approach to an issue. Her friend was astonished at how polite and kind Finucane remained in the face of some sustained provocation. 'You have to remember,' she would say, 'he pays my wages. If I didn't have the Irish listening public, I wouldn't have a job. I've chosen to put my life out in the public domain, so he has me in his kitchen every afternoon and he thinks he knows me. John and the children didn't, but I do, so I have to take the consequences.'

That meant having to put some thought into her clothes, which didn't go down well either. She loved to be well-dressed, she loved fashion, but the process killed her. I think part of it was to do with publicity – when people spotted her in Brown Thomas or somewhere and began with something like, 'Oh, Marian, here you are ...' it felt like a terrible intrusion. Another part of it was having her outfits dissected and priced. She was making a speech at a charity lunch one day and a nice woman came up to her and said, 'We've undressed you ... You got those shoes in so-and-so shop – they cost eighty-five. You got the skirt from such-and-such and that's a hundred and seventy-five.

And your jacket came from Richard Lewis.' It became so off-putting that she used to drive into the car park in Brown Thomas, sit in the car for five minutes, say, 'Ah, forget it,' reverse and drive out.

In the end, we came upon a little clothes shop in Rome that we returned to nearly every year. The clothes were good quality, made for tall women and reasonably priced, but the best thing for Finucane was that no one would ever know where they came from or how much they cost.

When tackled about her earnings, she often quoted Meryl Streep, who once said she would do the movies for free: the millions she got were for all the hassle. Finucane took the same view. She loved her job so much she would broadcast for free – but all the intrusion and commentary that went with it? You should get paid for that.

So, when Century arrived and began competing for the stars, it was timely to say the least. We believed their best strategy would have been to make their own stars, but who was going to turn their noses up at a battle that could only end well for people like Finucane?

She got round her squeamishness at talking about money by engaging a negotiator, Kieran Corrigan, who proceeded to frighten the life out of RTÉ and negotiated every contract thereafter. Years later, when they asked her to find another negotiator, saying the current one was awkward and difficult, she came home and told me with a laugh, 'Jaysus, he's doing his job well.'

It provided a healthy boost for our cash flow. With that and our liking for the unpredictable, we went out in the world to seek diversion and, I suppose, a kind of oblivion.

*

Our travels always began with some high-minded idea followed by a descent into chaos. The usual procedure was to acquire all the serious books on the history, politics and geography of our carefully planned destination and spend months reading up before compiling a fascinating and energetic itinerary for the expedition. Until we actually got there and got drunk on illegal brandy at the bottom of a hill and were wildly entertained while somehow missing the high-minded object of the entire exercise or mistaking a whole area for somewhere else.

I think at the heart of it all was our ability to rub along together and to find fun and diversion in situations where other travel companions, quite reasonably, might have flounced onto the next flight home.

We always set out to please each other. I remember

dishing up the Sunday dinner once – the usual roast beef, mashed and roast potatoes, turnips – and for some reason I looked at Marian and said, 'Do you know, I don't really like turnips.'

'Well, I hate turnips,' she said.

'So now you tell me, after all these years – I cooked them because I thought you loved them,' I said.

'And I only ate them because I thought you loved them,' she said.

They were off the menu within seconds.

My life with Finucane was made up of adventures, taking a daft idea and seeing what would happen to it. And that brought out the seekers in us, always nosing around for clues to how the world worked. Some of the crazy things we thought we should do lacked any rhyme or reason but often led into something else, a discussion or digression leading to another search.

Her curiosity about the world was limitless. When I brought her tea every morning, she would be watching the news on several channels – BBC and Al Jazeera among others. I confined myself to Al Jazeera. The main outlook was outward, to the world. The household radio ran on RTÉ analogue, drizzling away in the background, and over the morning tea the background noise from Finucane sometimes comprised a stream of curses, usually about someone who had uncritically taken a report off the wires that failed to present the full picture.

Sometimes, the full picture was too complex to describe in a single item, but it was also likely that Finucane had been in the place being described and knew the history. Quite often, she knew the players. She had a deep knowledge of many things but wore it very lightly. 'I listen for a living,' she would say endlessly. The truth was that she was incredibly well informed.

*

For our first serious trip way back when we first got together, I decided we should travel to see brown bears in the Balkans. In fairness to Finucane, the most easy-going woman in the world, she never balked.

We flew to the north of Italy, took the hydrofoil over to Dubrovnik, then headed up into the mountains of what was then Czechoslovakia. No sign of brown bears.

I was anxious for her to see some history, so in Dubrovnik I took her to the lamppost where a priest had been hung years before, and we talked to a man who felt, correctly, that the place was about to explode.

We had given up on the brown bears and were sunning ourselves one day when my body flared up and the swelling became so serious it closed my eyes.

'You're allergic to the sun,' said the local hospital doctor in excellent English.

'No, that's not possible. I've spent all my life in the sun – I love it,' I said.

'You're allergic to the sun,' he repeated, and gave me an infusion that reduced the swelling. Thus ended the Balkan history lesson.

After all those years, I discovered an allergy to UV light, a fairly serious affliction for a farmer and traveller who likes hot places. My white skin burns in the deserts and in North Mayo, and it burns where there is no smog. I developed a theory that it was smoking related, but an eminent doctor in a Dundee hospital linked it with stress and suggested that men around the age of 45 seemed particularly vulnerable to it. That sounded plausible, since Marian and I had just split up with our spouses. Now I slather myself with special cream and venture out with optimism.

Years later, being the ringleader in some of the madder stuff, I decided that we should go to Ladakh in Nepal, high up in the Himalayas, to witness a phenomenon that might or might not be rooted in reality. Levitating monks. I had a great desire to see them.

The bus we took to climb the Himalayas had never been serviced by the look of it but came festooned with reassuring images of the gods to protect the driver and passengers. The driver was an alarmingly contented man, chewing khat and singing away. Every time the bus rounded a bend on the gravel road, the back end leaned way out over the gorge, allowing us a panoramic view of the wrecks of buses, cars and trucks scattered way below. Not ideal for someone with Marian's fear of climbing heights.

We came to stretches where logs had been laid to replace the large chunks of road that had broken off and plummeted into the gorge. Approaching the first one, we watched keenly as a bus ahead of us negotiated the logs, and we noted that under the weight the logs all bent at an interesting angle towards the drop. So, I suggested to the bus driver that perhaps if all the passengers got out, it might reduce the weight and he would then drive across the logs and we would all get back on the bus alive and in one piece. No, he said, that would be bad luck. Marian and I held hands. At about two o'clock in the morning, we came to a halt at a station with three tin sheds.

It was black night. Across the road from us was a cave, and outside it, a huge brazier was burning brightly. We went inside and the driver gestured towards the women – 'You sleep in here, the men sleep over there.'

Finucane, for once in her remarkably tolerant life, did not just nod quiescently. 'It is the law in my country that I must sleep with my husband,' she said firmly.

The driver relocated us to the empty restaurant.

When we headed over to the brazier to get something to eat, twenty to thirty tribesmen had pitched up in the cave, all with long-barrel guns and knives hanging from their waists. Finucane was intrigued and started chatting to one of them as you do when you haven't a word of each other's language. His friends were riveted. Too late, I noticed that against the firelight her body was revealed in detailed silhouette under her thin sari – you could see what she'd had for her breakfast. I shot over to her. 'Marian, shut it and come in here at once. I could be at the bottom of that gorge while you're being landed in God knows bloody where,' I hissed.

'Why?' she asked.

'Because thirty men with big guns and knives are studying you very closely, and they like what they see.' That might have been an unfair summation of the company, but I didn't fancy our chances if it turned out to be true.

We ate our omelettes hastily and were ushered into our bedroom/restaurant by the driver, who locked the door and turned off the light from the outside and left us in total darkness to agitate about visiting snakes. If there were going to be snakes here, I reasoned, they were going to be in this room. They were going to come in from the cold through the holes under the floor and take a night's kip with us. Then again, we reminded ourselves, we always carried ampoules of serum for snakebite so it would be grand, probably.

We decided to sleep in one sleeping bag and put the other around us as an extra layer of protection and then to hold hands so that at least we would die together. The snakes never came but we held hands anyhow. Finucane and I held hands everywhere we went, all our lives. Everywhere. I can never remember us not holding hands.

Next morning, the bus finally wheezed into our destination and we settled into the guesthouse. I requested a drink from the proprietor. There was none, he said. Oh dear.

I gave ten rupees to a boy and asked him to go down to the village and find me some drink. He returned to say the cobbler had some for sale. It was a bottle of French brandy, seal unbroken, left by a tourist. We bought the whole bottle and took it back to bed.

After a few brandies and smokes, we fell into a deep sleep. When I woke up a few hours later, I was paralysed. I was quite sure I was dead and that the brandy was poisoned. A look at Marian confirmed it. 'Can you move any muscles?' I asked her.

'No,' she said.

Ambulances and hospitals seemed very far away from there. So, once more, we held hands – insofar as we could in that state – and waited to die.

Some hours later, movement mercifully returned. At some point it finally occurred to us that by puffing cigarettes and pouring brandy down our throats high up in the rarefied mountain air, we were forcing our hearts to work at manic rates, with the inevitable result.

In terms of mission objective, it all went downhill from there. Did we ever see the great levitation? I can only say that if it happened, the pair of us were somewhere in the vicinity, recovering from oxygen deprivation, slumped against a wall. Another Clarke–Finucane fiasco.

The threat of snakes loomed large in our imaginations, mainly because we roamed around places where they lived and we were terrified of them. Only our undying faith in the antidote ampoules we always carried gave us the courage to carry on.

Not long after the Himalayas journey, we were flying into Ecuador in pursuit of Bishop Eamonn Casey, who was fleeing from scandal and holed up in a convent there. We had a few other objectives for the trip. On the list was a look at the Panama Canal and the Mitad del Mundo in Ecuador, said to be the home of the centre of the earth for various technical and geophysical reasons. I thought we might also include some old sugar plantations. The only obstacle was any possible encounter with the fer-de-lance – a notoriously venomous eight-foot-long pit viper.

Before we set off, I was getting yellow-fever shots in a Dublin clinic and mentioned in passing the possibility of meeting with a fer-de-lance. The doctor blinked.

'We're grand,' I assured him. 'We have ampoules of serum.'

Looking sceptical, he asked to see them. Then he chucked them straight in the bin. 'They wouldn't stop a worm,' he said, 'never mind a fer-de-lance. And another thing: they're five years out of date.'

Faith is an interesting concept. Up to that point, Finucane and I believed we were immortal in the face of water moccasins, fer-de-lances and all their kin. For 10 years we had travelled in the belief that they couldn't touch us – because we were armed with this substance that wouldn't stop a worm. We never concerned ourselves with the efficacy of it or the expiry date, and that was partly due to the chaos that developed around – or by – us, we agreed, but it was more about faith, we decided, and how we come to believe things that have no basis in reality. Which led us all the way back to religions and myth, of course.

We gave the sugar plantations a miss on that trip.

*

My atheism was firmly grounded, but I had always been intrigued by the passage in the Book of Genesis about Moses crossing the Red Sea then leading the Hebrews across the Sinai desert for 40 years.

That gave rise to another notion. I thought it would be interesting to see why it took him so long. So we hired two horses, a jeep and a driver and rode across the desert for six days, galloping horses we could barely control in the baking desert, experiencing the remarkable Bedouin laws of hospitality and the odd polite cut-throat smuggler.

One danger of riding in the desert heat is that sweat evaporates instantly so you don't feel it, and therefore the risk of dehydration ratchets up for both horse and rider.

We tore up the flinty foothills and waved at a camel train whose master invited us to join them for tea. The master's son spoke English and they asked a lot of questions about what took us there. The women were making the tea, of course, and scraps of conversation floated over to where Marian was being told that only the boys go to schools. 'Marian,' I begged through gritted teeth, 'I know what your next question is and just don't. I could end up in a drain and you somewhere even less salubrious.' Feminism didn't chime with a lot of things in those parts, I reckoned, though she probably knew that. It was all part of the job while travelling with Finucane.

In South America, once I had crossed off one of my objectives – to see the Panama Canal – we attempted to head for south Ecuador and Bishop Casey, the main business of the trip. The region was wracked by storms. Four times the plane took off from the airport to climb the Andes, and four times the pilot had to turn back, descending towards the sea, and for 400 to 500 miles, we could see nothing below us but vast surfaces of water where there should have been farms and villages. Livelihoods, homes and vast acreages of crops were under metres of flood water.

What made it surreal was that each time we landed back in Panama we caught the international news on

CNN, where the entirety of it was the story of Gennifer Flowers and whatever distinguishing mark she had or hadn't identified on Bill Clinton's penis. For four days Bill Clinton's appendage was the news and it was on the fourth day, I think, that Clinton himself made a public appearance with a cleric alongside who was going to help guide him away from his wilful ways.

'What an extraordinary juxtaposition we have here,' I said to Marian. CNN's preoccupation – and America's – was whether Clinton had been playing away from home, so to speak. And here were we heading for south Ecuador to seek out another man who had been playing away from home and who was the preoccupation of the Irish news. Two men, caught breaking no law, both believing they were somehow protecting the magisterium of office by denying it all.

Finucane and I spent time pondering those matters. The magisterium of office, the magisterium of the Church, what does it mean? How many lies do you tell to protect a particular edifice? And how do you justify it in the context of the live human disaster we could see happening before us? The sheer devastation that we had witnessed and the world's eyes turned elsewhere. That was the media, and we were up to our necks in it.

Another favourite topic was how we learn to live in the

now. India, Finucane felt, was the place that seemed most amenable to it. She loved it above everywhere else.

On one Indian trip, we ended up sleeping for two nights on the chilly concrete among hundreds of people in a teeming railway station. For some reason, our attention was drawn to three young women who had got off the train with a baby. All they had was a small bag, and from it, they produced a few very cheap saris which they tied together in a circle. Then they looked up and down the platform, lay down in a circle joined together by the saris, placed the baby in the middle and went to sleep. The baby played for a while until he too fell asleep. If he tried to move or climb over the three women, he would wake them up. That image of perfect serenity burnt itself into Finucane's head.

They had no job, no money and probably no food, she said, yet they felt secure while we, the first-world folk, were fidgety, insecure, battering and fighting and striving, chasing security through armies, class and gender. What made people who had nothing feel so secure? Maybe they had learned to live in the now.

Or maybe they were simply resigned to the randomness of life.

*

When Marian offered me my trip of choice for my sixtieth birthday, of course I chose the Galápagos, Darwin's laboratory.

All of my interests combined in a fascination with Darwin. His story was a series of bizarre coincidences. He was a passenger on the HMS *Beagle* only because the reverend became ill, and such was the loathing between himself and the captain that he left the boat when they reached Argentina and made his way by mule up through South America to the Galápagos. Random to the core.

Finucane found a Russian boat to take us, carrying about sixty passengers of around nine nationalities.

In Chile, we watched as a group of eight young Japanese people that included a young man with callipers boarded our boat. A brave man, we thought; it would be a hard crossing in a big Pacific swell for someone unsteady on his feet. But he had attentive friends. Three of them always seemed to form behind him in a protective group.

Around fifty miles off the Galápagos, the captain made a surprising announcement. Two of the passengers were going to be married and we were all invited to the wedding. The groom turned out to be the young man with the callipers.

We were to assemble in the dining room at three o'clock, said the captain, and we should wear our best clothes – which at best would be a clean shirt. The groom arrived, then his bride with the group of friends. Following a Japanese ritual, she sat down and he stood beside her, and we watched in tense silence as the boat heaved and bucked and he was clearly fighting to stay on his feet. The best man stood close with one arm out, but we could sense the groom's fierce determination to do it alone and in our heads we were willing his body to remain upright – *stay standing, please stay standing*. The boat rocked in a huge swell and the captain read the required words with great deliberation – *hurry up, hurry up* – and declared he had the right to marry them under the law.

And finally, at last, he said, 'Will you, Passport Number 10730497, marry Passport Number 40358706?' I've invented the numbers, but this is what the captain did: he married two passport numbers. And all we could think was *please, please, keep it short*. The room was thick with tension. And then the captain said, 'You may kiss the bride.' The cheers and roars must have been audible 50 miles away. He then announced that Passport Number 10730497 had invited us all to the party.

The place was exploding with joy and excitement. Everybody was hugging everybody else, and we decided that each of the nationalities and the mainly Russian staff would sing a song for the couple. Marian and I sang 'Molly Malone' – or she sang and I growled – and we looked at each other, laughing and sobbing great floods of tears. Then we looked around and realised the whole room was laughing and crying, strangers pouring their hearts out in a surge of love, sharing moments of the purest joy and maybe some of the loss and grief that's within us all.

I try to analyse it now and think about words like 'collegiality', 'comradeship', 'love' and 'faith' above all. The fierce self-belief it took for that young man to remain standing for his wedding and our fierce, silent communal will spurring him on. It was one of the most extraordinary, joyful afternoons we had ever known. And beyond beautiful.

Marian lived for exactly this, for the humanity of the people she encountered, for all those extraordinary, unexpected moments when the world revealed itself in some new way. And for a while, I suppose, it took the edge off her grief.

*

Sinéad was never far away. Some years after her death, we were in Jerusalem and met Isaac, then a minister, the son of

Belfast-born Chaim Herzog, the sixth president of Israel, and himself a future president.

Isaac would have been well aware that Finucane and I had made repeated visits to Palestine and had a sound knowledge of the region's history. He had obviously done some research on us and, sometime later, made us an offer we could hardly refuse. A tree would be planted in Sinéad's memory on the Mount of Olives, the ancient Jewish burial site lying close to the Old City and across the Kidron Valley from the Temple Mount, where, according to scripture, the resurrection of the dead will begin and the messiah will appear.

The cynic in me questioned why this was happening, of course. But it is a rare honour to be remembered where so many of the venerable figures in Jewish history are buried.

We accepted the invitation and travelled to Jerusalem with Jack. A plot had been prepared, and Marian planted the tree in that beautiful place in a very simple, moving ceremony laden with symbolism. Tears flowed freely. Afterwards, a certificate was presented to Marian, describing the location of Sinéad's tree and its significance.

It is true that we could both be rather careless with such documents, in the same way that we never took photographs on our travels. Nothing needed to be documented; it was enough that we would remember. Yet even I was surprised when a recent search through old documents failed to yield that certificate. I wondered if Marian had given it for safekeeping to Mary Corbally, who has been working for us for 27 years and was very close to Marian. I was astonished to hear that Marian had never said a word to her about the tree or the certificate.

It's possible that Marian used it as a bookmarker and unintentionally lost sight of it. But it's more likely that she put it away somewhere obscure so she would never have to look at it again. She never wanted people to make an undue exception of her. She accepted honorary doctorates and thought the gesture was kind, but she would have questioned the premise because she genuinely believed she was no better or no worse than anyone else.

But I believe the missing certificate says something more significant about her complex relationship with Sinéad. That loss remained her cross, her hell, hers alone to bear, and external reminders cut into her soul. That tree and that moving ceremony on the Mount of Olives were buried deep in the iceberg and, like the certificate, never to be resurrected.

EIGHT

Drink

The hints are all there, I believe. You may have guessed that I am an alcoholic on the journey of a lifetime.

Alcoholism doesn't hit like a bolt from the blue: it leaches your life away over decades. I never knew who I was, and I'm not too sure I know who I am even now. The great thing about alcohol, I discovered, was that it gave me the freedom not to worry about it.

When I went into business at 19, I took to it like a duck to water. It was all about drinking and making a few bob, as far as I could see. And everyone else was doing it. From the age of 16 to 22 or 23, it was a rite of passage. Young men and young ladies got drunk: it was the craic, it was great, and it would never end.

There was falling around the place, waking up in strange houses, strange beds, strange places. Standard stuff.

No, sorry – standard stuff for the people I knocked around with. So, one assumed that everyone else was doing it. The only people who were not were the fellas who were into sport, and I was never interested in sport anyway.

The only limit on play was money. Why would you stop drinking if you had money? Making money came easily to me, so more money meant more drink. None of it prevented me going to work every day, bright and early. Increments of alcohol were imbibed as we went along, meeting clients for elevenses, for lunch, for dinner. Having a tipple, doing business, having a tipple, making money, having a tipple.

Being diagnosed as a 'functioning alcoholic' when I finally landed in St John of God's many years later was no surprise.

What 'functioning' meant in my case is that I remained relatively coherent while being removed from reality. I was always in the office at eight o'clock in the morning, so it seemed as if I was functioning. In the later stages, that would have entailed a stop by a Smithfield early house on the way for four or five halves of whiskey.

You are doing what you should be doing, and you firmly believe that part of your brain that insists you are thinking straight. What you are actually doing is floating and thinking, 'I'll sit here for a while longer and have another drink. There's something I need to do now, and I'll definitely do it – whenever.' In my rear-view mirror, life is a blur.

I didn't spend time taking out old resentments and polishing them, as many alcoholics do, because I never had enough resentments to bring out and polish. Musing about whether I could defy gravity and fly would have been far more interesting.

I was functioning as an alcoholic in one sense. The decisions you make in that mode may well be correct – up to a point. It's the great what-if. Take the Smithfield fiasco. I had done something quite prescient: bought a site and commissioned the first small office block in that area. Did I make any glaring mistakes? I didn't think so. But what if I had been sober – would I have caught some of the architect's errors or approached the project differently? Undoubtedly.

Hindsight is wonderful and it's also a waste of time.

I also invested – or gambled – in projects that sounded crazy but made lots of money. I ran the farm and the production company for Marian's various business activities, managed the household and oversaw major renovations at various properties. We had kitchen-table chats or conferences almost daily, wrote scripts for documentaries and programmes, kicked around ideas for the column she wrote for *Women's Way* magazine and I helped her to craft it – all while drunk to some degree or other. I even wrote a play that may have won a prize. I never knew, and I don't know to this day, what was in it, who the characters were or what it was about. I remember only the name: *The Wounded Armadillo*.

It's always difficult to judge the cross-over point between heavy drinking and the realisation that you can't survive without it. I think that shift happened when we moved to Mullingar.

Once Marian had gone to work, I'd get out the bottle of whiskey and drink half of it, wander around the farm with Sinéad running along beside me, come back and drink the other half, then fall asleep. Here was a place where I could have a few without intrusion or accountability.

In later years, I was probably up to two or three bottles a day, and two things happened, I believe. I couldn't function without whiskey, and I couldn't think without it. Everything ceased to matter except drink. Marian would arrive home and find me flat on the sofa, drunk. I'd gab away happily.

'You're drunk,' she'd say.

'No, I'm not, I've only had a couple of drinks.'

I was living in a bizarre alcohol-fuelled world of my own and really had no idea who I was.

'Jesus, you'd want to watch the drink,' Marian would say. Now, this was a house full of drink and we drank a lot together. She could match me whiskey for whiskey, so I could defend myself on that basis. The major difference was that if I went out with Marian for a drink somewhere, I'd already have a bottle or two in me. She had a great capacity for alcohol, but she also had discipline around her work. She had to be on the road to Dublin by 6.30 a.m.

She was immensely tolerant in spite of regular provocation. Towards the end of our time in Reynella House, I lost my licence for six months for drink-driving. At another stage, we were about to seal a deal, a very important one for both of us that we had spent a long time setting up. When I arrived for the meeting clearly a bit the worse for wear, she took a long, cold look. 'You're drunk. You can't do this deal drunk. It's too important. I'm going to say I have another appointment and we'll leave.' That was the first time I had seen her really, really angry: what I was doing had now interfered with the business of the day.

Of course, she must have been biting her tongue for a long time. She knew all the people that I knocked around with were, if not full-blown alcoholics, steadily on the road to it. But that was also the sort of society that a part of her had to buy into. There was another compartment of her life that was also suffused with alcohol, one that involved journalists, broadcasters, political guys and religious guys she mixed with. In many ways, she had two separate lives, though she only had to live in mine.

How much she bottled up for my benefit, I really don't know.

Every alcoholic knows deep inside themselves that something is seriously awry. I made countless attempts to get off alcohol on my own. An old friend in AA tried to help me. I went cold turkey a few times and would manage to stay dry for three days or four, hanging on, hanging on …

I had a lot of real battles with myself. *Today you're going to work*, I'd swear. I would make it as far as half eleven, maybe twelve. Around six months after Sinéad's death, I was admitted to the Rutland Centre, where I lasted for a few days and left.

What was driving this spiral? I think in my case it was guilt – with myself. I wasn't connected to the world. My life was lived through liquor. I was gone, floating above reality. I was lost but couldn't say what I was lost from. It was just a deep sense of emptiness and isolation. Delve below that, analyse it for those things that made me tense and vulnerable to temptation – or what I call the thought before the thought of lifting a glass – and the only answer that ever made any sense to me was low self-esteem. A lot of low self-esteem.

That may surprise readers having read about my childhood years.

There's no doubt a lot of alcoholics have experienced serious childhood trauma. I know this from 30 years' experience of listening. Alcoholism, according to current thinking, is mainly about things that happened in your youth and teenage years, and many alcoholics I meet have suffered violence of some kind in their childhood – parental violence, incest, every kind of sexual depravity. I've also met many who believe their alcoholism was inherited, because most of them had a parent who was an alcoholic.

My theory is that as children they had experienced a terrible existential anxiety – *Where is Daddy? Will he come home? Will he break a window or throw the frying pan at me?* – which they suppressed with alcohol as they got older. Then when they went through the process of becoming sober, it slowly emerged that something had happened when they were quite young.

That left me with a conundrum because none of that applied to me as far as I could see. I had a terribly happy childhood and great teenage years. I had loving, tolerant parents who drank a glass of stout from time to time. There was a confidence that came with that easy family life, even if you didn't say things like that back then. There was fun. There was always that certainty of family and stability.

We weren't well-off but we had tremendous privilege and assumptions. I know the difficulties of being a teenager, but they were fairly standard in my case – too small, too this, too that, girls don't like me – so what was I moaning about?

I have examined every part of my life and come back every time to that lack of self-esteem, that sense of failure.

I believe I was a disappointment to my parents. Get a child to a certain age and you can sense the parental brain whirring – *Oh Lord, if you don't get to this level or you don't do that, you'll be left behind, a loser*. They wouldn't have said those words, of course, but it would probably have been implied that I had failed in some way. And I *had* failed. I felt that myself.

I spent years looking for a cause and I could only see the negatives in me. *You didn't do this and you didn't do that, you broke ranks, you should have become a lawyer or a chemist or a civil servant or something that is the acceptable version of success in this society.*

It preoccupies you in strange ways. I say to myself, *You could have done this or that with your eyes closed – so why didn't you do it?* Low self-esteem. *Is that true?* Maybe.

Whatever it was, it left me with a dangerous lack of purpose. I'm struck by the fact that giving up drink for a month before donating the bone marrow for Sinéad really didn't present a huge problem for me, a very serious drinker. The explanation seems obvious to me now. I had a clear purpose and the cause was vital.

But when that procedure was over, the purpose vanished. I was left, I think, with an even greater sense of entitlement to reach for the whiskey again and I used it.

Sinéad's death gave me 'permission'. On the day of her funeral, I remember Deirdre Purcell asking would I like to go for a walk, and I guessed that Marian had asked her to 'keep an eye on him'.

'Who's setting me up?' I asked.

The move to Kilteel hadn't eased the craving for or the availability of alcohol. The very slow rebuilding of the Flurry Knox house just meant I had pub companions on tap in the shape of the builders. At around noon, the lads and I would repair to the Kilteel Inn to discuss how mullions are installed in windows or something, then return to work around five and decide to adjourn.

Marian was clearly worried. I recall holding court with various people in the Shelbourne one evening and suddenly noticing something. 'You're drinking me whiskey,' I said to her.

'I've been drinking it for the last three months to try and keep you half-sober,' she replied.

The woman I loved was drinking for me to protect me? That should have been a wake-up call.

She had tried to rein me in – or, more accurately, she had tried it our way, fairly persistently but quietly, in that peculiar way of not crossing into each other's private space, never arguing, never raising our voices, maybe too swift, I think, to sweep away issues that were contentious and threatened the magic.

That was why her ultimatum, when it came, must have erupted from the depths of her soul. It crashed through all the barriers of our individual privacy, of being independent bodies, independent lovers, making up our own minds, never criticising each other.

'Why don't you go to Mayo and drink yourself to death with your mates? I don't want to hang around watching you kill yourself, which is what you're doing.' She was firm, cool and aloof. And she was probably shaking inside.

She had come into a world which was so different to any she had envisaged or imagined, and she was much younger than I. But Finucane had a tough core and huge moral courage. When she set her sights on what she thought was the proper way, the lady was not for turning.

I knew I was way out of control. Deep inside I knew I was in trouble – for me, never mind for anyone around me. It may sound self-pitying, but alcoholics become terribly lonely. I could be in a crowd of my friends and with Marian, whom I adored, having interesting conversations, but my head would be somewhere else, isolated, cut off. I wasn't there.

When I try to reflect on those years, I know I wasn't present at important times for my family. I'm not even there in my own memory quite often. Like almost every alcoholic, I suffered blackouts and often have to rely on others to remind me of incidents. The last straw of many last straws, I believe, involved some incinerated pizza which I tried to foist on Jack after school. He refused it, quite rightly, while I was insisting in a manner and volume unheard of in our house. I might have been a sloppy drunk but never an angry one. Nuala O'Faolain once said I was the happiest drunk she'd ever met, except that I had verbal diarrhoea – but now this happy drunk had crossed a line.

Having upended the household, I fell asleep in the kitchen. Marian hadn't yet returned from work. But the word had gone out, and when I woke up, the warrior Nell was standing before me. She had left instructions that she was to be disturbed by nobody.

'You're a fucking alcoholic,' was her opening barrage. Nell and I had known each other for a long time and were very close. 'You're going to lose her, you know,' she said.

'Yeah, I get that impression,' I said.

'Anyhow, you're killing yourself.'

'I know.'

'Right, when are you going [to rehab]?'

'I'll think about it.'

'No. No good – when are you going?'

'Tuesday.'

'Why don't you go now?'

She and I were in conclave for six hours or so, I believe. At about ten o'clock, she invited Marian to join us in the kitchen and asked Kathleen to pack a bag for me.

Marian was terrified that I wouldn't go. I went.

*

'Jesus, you had a great run at it,' a facilitator said almost admiringly in St John of God's.

I was in my sixties.

I was terrified, but a hazy part of me was weak with relief as well. Somebody was going to look after me, it wasn't my problem any more, I was lost but there were people there who knew how to solve this.

First, a three-day stopover for a detox in St Michael's Hospital. Then the taxi arrived for St John of God's and we were speeding past familiar old pubs – 'Will you stop for a moment ...?'

'No,' he said.

Going through the doors I felt the 'failure' sign flashing on my forehead. *You couldn't do it on your own*, said the needling voice in my head. Where had I lost it? Where had it all gone wrong? What was I in for now?

I had a few panic attacks. 'Jesus, I never fed the cattle.'

'That's all right, we'll look after them,' Marian said.

I thought of other urgent matters, anything to get me out of there. 'God, I never got in touch with Paddy now, and I meant to do that, maybe I'll just give him a shout.'

'No, that's all right,' Marian said.

And then, over a few days, a kind of muzzy clarity descended.

In a class of 23 there were two guys I knew. One asked me how I was feeling.

'Fucking awful,' I said.

'We slip across to Boland's pub every evening – do you want to come?'

'No,' I said. No. For once in my life, I said no.

That encouraged me. Because what they do in rehab is hold up a mirror. That's all. Your job is to take a long look at yourself. I'd cleared the first hurdle. I'd handed my problem over and was feeling strangely positive.

Reality check: you go into rehab as a heavy drinker and you come out of it an alcoholic. In the process, I discovered a whole part of me which I had denied.

Marian came in every night and talked as if there was nothing out of the ordinary, even though I was in an institution. I would tell her what went on that day and how I felt. She knew a lot about alcoholism because she had done endless programmes on it.

'Well, you know I'm doing this for you,' I said to her one day – the one thing you shouldn't say, I speedily discovered.

'No, you're not – you're wasting your time if you're doing it for me. You're doing it for yourself – and be very clear on that,' she said firmly.

The journey towards sobriety is long and hard and

entails a lot of brutal honesty with yourself. There was an inquisitor – as I called the poor counsellor – who used to ask, 'Well, how are you feeling now?'

'Ah, grand,' I'd say. (Feeling like shit, actually.)

'Do you really mean that?'

'Ah, no.'

'So, what do you mean?'

'Jesus, why are you probing into my private life? Why are you asking me that?'

Had I been a bad person? Well, I hadn't murdered anyone. I was slaughtering myself now and for good reason – I was also beginning to get agonising glimpses of how Marian and other family members and friends around me had suffered.

I have no doubt that it was a terrible period in Marian's life. She compartmentalised it – which she was very good at – but she certainly wasn't happy. All the excitement and the adventures paled in the shadow of alcohol because she never knew when she came home whether she had me or whether she didn't – 'I can never be sure what I'm going to meet when I get home.' Her sense of internal security was damaged. The magic had gone cool. My magic had gone cool.

But she would never talk about it.

I tried to tell her that I understood now.

'It must have been really terrible,' I'd start. 'I know now how bad I was, so thanks for sticking by me.'

'Ah, well,' she'd say – code for *Please don't question me. Don't make me talk about this*. Or she'd say, 'It was a bad period ...' Then, 'What did you do today?' although she knew already, in detail. Anything to move it on. The subject was buried deep in the Finucane iceberg, in that pot of grief and loss.

The family therapy sessions were tortuous. They ventured too far into her privacy, I think.

Facilitator: 'Well, how was that for you?'

Marian: 'All right.'

Facilitator: 'Did he turn up or not turn up?'

Marian: 'Ah, I can't remember.' She could remember all right.

The truth was that this 'functioning alcoholic' had turned up for things all the time. Pissed. Or at least half-pissed. A huge capacity for whiskey is not a great plan, my old friend Sam Sherling used to say, and he was right. But I was one of the hard men, or so I thought.

It was the ability to float. I was running a business and, apart from a period towards the end when I was patronising the early houses, I was in my office every morning at eight.

I had energy to burn and was bubbling with ideas. *Will we do this? Will we do that? Will we travel here? Did you ever think about looking at the Raj? Did you ever think …?* And when I wasn't doing that, we were bookworms, reading and sipping and drinking. It was our greatest pastime. Our other partner in reading and sipping and drinking was Nuala O'Faolain. We had this wine-drinking library. And I was an early riser, as any guest would tell you, bright eyed, attentive, happy to chat away while making the breakfast.

That family session, I think, was the most embarrassing time for Marian. I told her she didn't have to subject herself to it – 'You know and I know what went on.' When it was suggested in a general context that some of the women – and they were mainly women – should join Al-Anon, it went down like a lead balloon.

I look at life rather differently now than when I was 20, 30 or 40, obviously. I still have most of the values I started off with, but it's been quite a journey. The loneliness of an alcoholic brings tremendous isolation.

I was surrounded by people – and by people who loved me. And I loved them. But I wasn't there. *Is that all there is?* I used to wonder. Most recovering alcoholics at some point will talk about that particular quality of isolation and loneliness, how they felt completely out of sync with their families, first of all, and to a certain extent with the rest of the world. But was it just the alcohol?

There was a lot of dancing around this topic. I used to say to people, 'Jesus, if you had my problems, you'd understand why I drank.' Then one day a thought occurred – *What problems have I got?*

OK, I said to myself, *write down all your problems now and we'll take a look*. I couldn't think of any. All those years I had been hanging on to this idea that no one else had my problems and sure what could I do but drink?

I asked a counsellor once if I should see a psychologist about my youth. He said it would cost a fortune, would have to go back to potty-training years and might not even dredge up the answer. For me, it was the best advice in the circumstances because it allowed me to say to myself – and believe it – *Whatever you did or didn't do, whatever you did wrong, whatever the low self-esteem, whatever it was, then so be it. Now get on with your life.*

The solution lay with me. One of the things I figured out was that I never lived in the now. I lived over the moon, down the road, way over there. I'd have a hundred ideas before I got out of bed. I was very impressed with the White Queen, who had at least six impossible ideas before breakfast. She could have been one of my mentors.

I had to get grounded somehow. But how do you do that when you have no sense of who you are or what you should be doing?

I had no interest in accumulating wealth, even when it was happening. What was I doing this for? What was the purpose of that? Maybe it went back to reading – or misreading – the existentialists at 15. I never had any sense of purpose. All the things that are recommended for an up-and-coming businessman, like, say, joining a golf club? Not for me. Many alcoholics I know are religious. But if you decide that society is a myth, if you decide that religion is a myth, if you decide there is no purpose in life – all of which I had indeed decided – what do you lean on? How do you cope? Does anything matter?

I had cut myself adrift from the normal support systems that anchor people's lives, and I really hadn't found any alternative except alcohol.

So, what do you look towards?

It was about then, believe it or not, that the Angelus bells came into play. It was a strange one for someone absolutely opposed to the normal props of most people's lives, such as religion. But I realised at some point that my head could be in Timbuktu but the Angelus bells would always stop me in my tracks – that pause that triggered a few simple questions: *OK, what are you thinking now? Where are you going? What are you doing? What's the purpose?*

What clinched the path ahead for me was the last meeting in St John of God's. Professor Tubridy was having a 'How are you all doing now?' conversation, and he laid out the odds: 'There are twenty-four of you in this group; fifty per cent of you will be back drinking before the end of the year. One of you will die. By year two, two to three of you will be dead.' And finally: 'Of the remaining fifty per cent, thirty per cent will be back drinking.'

Meaning what? At a rough guess, about four of us in this room might make it through. That was the message. At the end of his talk, we all began to look at each other and wonder *Who's dead? Who's going back? Who'll make it?*

The chances were so shockingly tiny that I asked him later if he was sure about those figures. He had been doing this for 30 years, he said, and for the first 10 years, it had totally frustrated him. They were using best practice, yet the figures never changed. The Swedish system had one of the best alcoholic treatment programmes going, yet the outcomes were the same. After 10 years he had stopped getting frustrated, he told me. 'We tell participants: the chances of success are two per cent to three per cent. If you go to AA, that goes up by another two per cent. So, you get five per cent.'

I made a vow then that I would go to AA. I still do, every week.

*

All the AA steps after the first three are to help you find ways to protect yourself from alcohol. If you have something in your head that drives you to do this or that behaviour, get it out there, get rid of it and come to terms with it. Then you have a reasonable chance of making it.

My first forays into AA were non-starters. It all seemed very strange, embarrassing and irritatingly repetitive. I wanted to hide in a corner, and I certainly didn't want to speak. In desperation, I rang a friend from the advertising world and said I was trying to figure out this AA thing.

'Yeah, about time,' said Paddy.

'But I can't make head or tail of it,' I told him. 'I don't know what they're talking about. They seem to be moaning about this, that and the other, and nobody's talking about drink – they're talking about how they feel, for pity's sake.'

'Right, be in Hume Street AA, eight o'clock tonight, and I'll introduce you to some fellas you might like,' Paddy said.

We talked for a long time that evening. 'Be in Sandymount tomorrow night, eight o'clock,' Paddy said. And so it continued.

It wasn't enough to find a meeting and say we're all in it together. That's part of it, but we are from different walks of life, different classes, different establishments. You have to look at your own life and say why, what, who, where, what am I? I respected Paddy because he was one of the lads, he'd been through the mill, and he was no holy joe. He didn't carry a big public flag for sobriety. I had found my team, I suppose you could say.

Paddy told a story about having to go to a wedding sober for the first time. Sober makes you feel such a spare, and feeling spare makes you edgy. His gaze fell on a gregarious priest who was going from table to table, greeting everybody and chatting, taking the odd sip from the glass of wine in his hand. Paddy couldn't take his eyes off him, going around and around and around with the one glass, not even taking a proper glug from it. The priest finally got to Paddy's table – 'How is everybody here?' – and all Paddy could see was the wine, still, unbelievably, in the glass, and it was burning a hole in Paddy's head. 'Drink the fucking thing!' he blurted.

This was Paddy in early recovery, Paddy who was now

mentoring me and who probably saved my life.

I had a lot of friends who had lived the good life with me and who luckily got to AA and stayed sober. They surrounded me now. I would ring them and tell them I was going to a wedding the next week. 'Right, where is it? We'll meet you an hour before it – or two hours after it.' Or they would ring me because they needed support and I would help to surround them.

For the first six months after I got sober, Marian was very tentative about having a drink near me. A couple of weeks after I came out of rehab, I said to her, 'You're to continue drinking because otherwise it would be wrong. You like a drink. Why would you stop drinking for me? Your drinking won't stop or start me – it'll be me who stops and starts. So have your glass of wine.'

But we were very careful with each other in those early months. And then, like a lot of recovering alcoholics, I became the chauffeur on our nights out. Which is something most AA people do anyway.

Marian hated Christmas, but there were many parties to attend and I would drive. Occasionally, in case she failed the morning breathalyser tests, I would drive her into RTÉ while she scrabbled around for an aspirin. And it occurred to me one morning that I couldn't even remember having a hangover. I just threw another drink in and never allowed the hangover to intrude.

I called into a good friend's house recently at around ten o'clock in the morning and he was having his breakfast. Toast and a boiled egg. His wife and I had been to various AA meetings together and we were chatting.

'See the boiled egg he's eating? That's my penance. I give him a boiled egg every day,' she said.

'I never knew that was your penance,' said the husband.

'You're not supposed to know. This is me making amends for all the trouble I caused you, so I boil you an egg every morning.'

AA people work in mysterious ways.

*

What could I do to make amends to Marian? I loved her more. I wasn't sure how I could show her – except when she arrived home any day, any time, I was sober. And that, I presume, was a great gift to her, even at that late stage in our lives. There's a kind of arrogance in that, I know, but it made her life easier. She used to get fed when I wasn't drunk, because I did almost all the cooking, but when I was drunk she would come home dog-tired after a day's work and the long drive down to Mullingar and find me dozing with the kids on the sofa, watching some aimless television. Then she'd have to go and cook.

That never happened again.

It opened up a whole series of wonderful parts of my life with Marian. I ran all our domestic arrangements, and I was glad to run them. From my perspective, and I think from hers – though you never know – we ended up with a much deeper understanding of each other than we had before.

I was a very flawed scenario, I was discovering, but trying my damnedest to do better.

Afterwards, our survival strategy, I think, was to withdraw a bit from our old social life, partly by accident but more by design. We were living down the country, which precluded a lot of the Dublin craziness. We were much more settled. We went to events with me as chauffeur, drinking non-alcoholic beer, while Marian curtailed her drinking naturally. Maybe there is an age element too, where the body can't tolerate the quantities any more.

The stupidity of so much of my life, in terms of alcohol, was also laid bare. I realised I could serve up the gin and tonics, sit down with a group of people who were drinking, and it didn't bother me in the least.

Sobriety didn't just hand me back a life: it gave me back the sense of being alive, which is a different thing. I started to get excited about all sorts of ideas and interests. I love developing a curiosity about something and taking it to the edge to see what might happen.

I had almost thrown all that away.

It was a steep and difficult learning curve, but it was a huge liberation. Everything I did that was a bit daft was at least being done with a rational brain, or as rational as my brain gets.

I handled the social side of sobriety by immediately letting it be known I was an alcoholic. AA membership has to remain anonymous, for obvious reasons, but up to recent times it could have got you fired. Men and women – especially women – felt they had to hide it. I didn't have that problem, so I made a decision to tell everybody straight out that I was an alcoholic – then if they insisted on trying to buy me a drink, it was their problem. Only one person said to me, 'Ah, Jesus, that's terrible – you know, just drink a little,' or 'Just have one glass of white wine.'

'No, I'm a piss artist, leave it.'

'No, John, you're dead right, you're a piss artist.' Which was true. And then it was out there.

I can't be an AA mentor because I could be a long way

away when needed by someone in extremis, but I have a phone full of people who ring me when they're in trouble. I counsel a lot of alcoholics on the AA helpline, and I attend a lot of meetings. I'm the go-to man in my area when a distressed wife says, 'Would you ever talk to Jim? He's drinking too much.'

At the start of the pandemic, AA asked me to man one of the phones and I was delighted to do it. There are three of us between Naas, Newbridge, Rathcoole, Blessington, Clane and a few other places, and I get four or five calls a week from people who are in trouble. The level of violence and of drinking took a notable turn during Covid.

The callers are always apologetic. They're hurt and in pain and feel a sense of failure because they've slipped. The one thing they all say is 'I just thought of a drink and I had one.'

'But that's not true. What were your thoughts before you thought of the drink? Tell me what you thought, what upset you, what got to you, because by the time you "just thought" of a drink you were already gone or three-quarters of the way there.'

'Jesus, I don't know.'

'Well, you'd better think about that.'

'It was the cold, or the husband was this and that,' they'll say. They need a soul to talk to, someone to say they've just had a slip and remind them that nearly everyone has a slip. My job is give them back their confidence and get them back to AA.

I've swung close myself and I never get complacent. On the night of Marian's funeral, I went to an AA meeting.

How we bury our dead and the rituals surrounding death are important. People turn up and say lovely things, but what can you possibly say to a bereaved person who is lost and grieving? I never know what to say that's coherent, that means anything, that touches somebody. The best thing you can do, I think, is give them a hug.

There were many hugs and kind, loving exchanges at Marian's funeral, but AA was the only place where I felt everyone would instinctively understand the frustration and pain, the kind of self-blaming and the self-questioning of the alcoholic that culminates in the danger moment: the thought before the thought.

They say that soldiers who fought in a war, even on opposite sides, communicate in a different way with each other than people who haven't been in the battle. And it could be said that alcoholics have been in some wars, mainly with themselves. If they're in AA, it has probably been a painful gestation period of realisation. You're not who you thought you were after all. So who are you? What moves you? What makes you act in a certain way?

That night, there were eight old lags like me in the room, and I told them I needed to talk. I needed to talk, I said, to people who understood things like loss and how depression comes on you and the thought of a drink is suddenly there. So, I talked about Marian.

At the end of the hour, they said, 'We'll go home with you.'

'You don't need to – it's over now,' I said.

When I got home, the boys were still having a few drinks and something else was going on, I sensed. I spotted Neal going out of the house with a suspicious-looking package and realised they were hiding away all the whiskey and the brandy. Just in case.

'Neal, it's OK now. It's over.'

It really is OK. Because I have the old lags, the sort of granddaddies of the Rathcoole Drunkards' Association, who are on a similar wavelength to mine. And for six weeks at least after Marian died, four or five of them rang me every day – 'How are you? Are you worried? Didn't see you at the meeting? Would you like a cup of tea? Are you OK?'

'Yeah, I'm OK.' And because I know them, I know their concern. I hear one of their voices asking, 'How are you today, John?' I say, 'I'm grand,' – and I mean it.

So, I dodged that one.

Stuck with the programme.

Today, I'm not tearing my hair out wondering who I am – or not so much, anyway.

I can only sing the praises of AA.

NINE

Africa

Sometimes you look for connection where there is none. I can see how it might look to outsiders: John finds sobriety in his sixties, has time on his hands, and suddenly Finucane and he are roaming around South Africa with a white-saviour complex.

It's true that my liberation from alcohol moved me onto a very different plane, but there was no conscious decision that I recall. It was a random series of things that happened. The only connection is that they happened to resonate with the way we lived, the way we travelled, the way we thought and what we had seen. Every experience that you have in life arises from different emotions. They bring you to a place that opens something up, moves you forward to a different look at the world.

The spark that set us on the road to South Africa was an invitation from the South African government to come and have a look around the country. Every year they picked two journalists from somewhere in the world, and it was entirely open. That was its appeal. The chosen ones could travel anywhere they chose, see anything they liked, talk to anyone they wanted. They could spend a few weeks just admiring the scenery and playing golf if that's all they wanted to do.

The connection that created the spark was Melanie Verwoerd, the South African ambassador to Ireland in 2001, who gave her first radio interview to Marian. Marian asked her about the 1994 elections. By the time Melanie had finished an emotional description of the massive queues, how people had waited for days to vote and how older citizens were pushed to the polling booths in wheelbarrows, Finucane was staring at her intensely with tears in her eyes. It was not what the ambassador had come to expect during media interviews. Marian was listening *and* feeling.

Melanie had a hunch about Finucane, and it was this: she would always want to be more than just a tourist. She could be relied upon to dig deeper, to ask more questions, to try to get to the heart of a problem. With Finucane there would always be that extra 'But why …?' and the same ferocious curiosity would apply whether it was in a Bedouin camp, a studio encounter with a slippery businessman or a South African child.

When the itinerary was being drawn up, Finucane said she wanted to see the sights, of course, but she listed two other things specifically: she wanted to stay in a township for a night – an unprecedented request then – and she wanted to visit an orphanage for children with HIV/AIDS.

I was included in the package. Being a deeply shy person, when she was going anywhere Marian would often say, 'Please come with me – I can hide behind you.' She used to say the same to five-foot-two-inch Nell, who didn't quite camouflage her six-foot-one-inch frame in heels. What she wanted, really, was more of a front-of-house person. Then once the ice was broken with Finucane, of course, you couldn't get her out of the place. Anyway, I was with her on the trip to South Africa in June 2002.

For us, the trip was a conjunction of timing, events and circumstances. I have no doubt that it was the spirit of Sinéad that drove our first efforts there. Everything that Finucane and I had learned and experienced in our lives and on our travels found a resonance there, and Sinéad was chief among those. I believe Marian was not going to live out her life without some form of meaningful monument to our daughter's existence.

For our township-overnight, we were billeted in Khayelitsha, just outside Cape Town, and it was pretty obvious to me why no one had asked to stay there before. The homes were mostly tin-roofed shacks; there was one water tap and one toilet – out on the road – for a hundred people and a sense of menace in the air. We stayed with lovely hosts who fed us food we didn't recognise, and our bedroom was a haven for mosquitoes and other creatures. When something that looked very like a rat shot up the wall, Finucane dived under the blanket.

Later, I went out for a smoke where the man of the house was watching his daughters practising their harmonies for the church choir. It was a picture of sweet, peaceful domesticity.

'Lovely children,' I said.

Yes,' he answered. 'It's very hard to keep them here with all the child rape that's going on.'

We were aware of the myth that sex with a virgin was a 'cure' for AIDS. Nonetheless, it was shocking to hear it brought so close.

'I'm the chief necklacer,' he added as a matter of interest.

The local hangman in other words. When a child rapist was caught, the standard punishment was 'necklacing'. A tyre filled with kerosene was pulled down over the accused's chest and arms and set alight.

And our host was in charge.

I was back in bed trying to sleep when Marian woke me triumphantly. She had walked all the way through the township out to the communal toilet on the road and was beaming with achievement at her solo run.

Our next stop after Khayelitsha was a convent in white Cape Town where children infected with HIV/AIDS – an incurable disease then, with no treatment available – were being nursed. Pippa Shaeffer, an Englishwoman married to a South African lawyer, introduced us to the nuns who were doing this remarkable work. It was the little brass plaques on the wall, erected in memory of each child who had died, that stirred something deep in our souls.

Children were all around us, playing and chattering, and it was evident that a lot of them were dying. Many also had mothers who were dying of HIV/AIDS, but they were effectively separated because the women couldn't afford the bus fare to white Cape Town. The solution to that, said Sister Sandra, the Scottish reverend mother, was to build a children's hospice in Khayelitsha where the mothers could be with them to the end.

'Let's build one,' I said to Marian on the way home.

'How?' she asked.

'I don't know,' I said, 'but we're certainly capable of running card games and pub quizzes.' We could use her good name to raise funds and combine that with my business and organisational skills to get the building off the ground. And I always had a strange addiction to cement.

The following night, she had an event at An Cosán, where she presented the prizes every year. I went along as usual and was placed next to Liz O'Donnell, who turned out to be the minister of state for overseas development assistance and human rights. This was all news to me, since I didn't follow Irish politics. Was she in the business of giving money away? I asked.

She was indeed, she said. If we were to raise money, could we build a hospice in Khayelitsha and would she match us euro for euro? I asked. She said yes. A few days later, she introduced us to Brendan Rogers, the can-do person we needed, a man whose experience with the UN Development Programme and Irish overseas aid in Africa proved indispensable.

We told them about the children's hospice in the township and said we might add a day-care facility next door for the healthy children of mothers who were dying, all for €150,000. Our ambitions were mushrooming by the day. We were no white saviours; rather, we were getting a crash course in the catastrophic effects of HIV/AIDS on the social and family structures of South Africa and, to our shame, were only beginning to realise we had access to resources that many others did not. Marian's connections and mine formed a web of overlapping affluent circles – it was simply a matter of pulling them together. The Celtic Tiger was roaring, and people were primed for chats about social responsibility and giving something back.

Around a week after meeting Brendan Rogers, Finucane and I were at a dinner party in Tipperary with Mattie Ryan – the legendary jeweller who gave huge momentum to the North Tipperary hospice movement – regaling the guests with stories about our trip to Africa and the things we saw and did and, oh, by the way, we're going to build this hospice and we need to raise a substantial sum of money ...

'I'll help you there,' said a man at the table, quietly. We thanked him and went home, never expecting to hear another word from him because – as Finucane pointed out – there was a lot of drink taken.

But in my own new-found state of sobriety, I had noticed he wasn't drinking either, and I had his name and number. Next day I rang him and said his offer was far too generous, but if he had a couple of thousand to spare, we would be very grateful. A few days later, a generous donation arrived and, coupled with other donations, some big, some small, we were on our way.

True to her word, Liz O'Donnell matched what we raised euro for euro, whereupon Marian rang Melanie, the ambassador, and met her for lunch. 'So, I have the money,' she said. A few months later, in what Melanie called a wonky marquee, we had a grand opening of the new facilities, which the children celebrated by singing 'Molly Malone'. The Friends in Ireland charity was born.

*

It is impossible in a single chapter to describe or encapsulate our twenty-year roller coaster in the tribe lands of South Africa. We landed up in the midst of a full-blown deadly pandemic – HIV/AIDS – in a very new country. South Africa had been built around a population of three million (whites) and, with the ending of apartheid in 1994, now had 39 million people with completely inadequate social services, inadequate infrastructure and inadequate skills from the politicians downwards. The world knew very little about HIV/AIDS then, only that it was sexually transmitted and was fatal without the proper medications and care.

When Sinéad died we were lost, we had lost our fight, we had lost a daughter. A dreadful feeling of emptiness with no respite. For some reason, and I can't tell you what the reason was, I don't know or can't remember, I would tell you if I could, we decided to go to Auschwitz. As you walk through the halls that held the children's toys and mountains of black and blond children's hair that had been shaved off before they were euthanized, this vision has to be the abomination of abominations and yet in some bizarre way it gave us solace. Our daughter had died with love. We then took the taxi to Birkenau, which was an upscaled model for killing. In other words, it could cope with more deaths more effectively. We stood at the gates, looked at each other and said, 'We've had enough.' This had to be the final moment of our despair.

Healing seems to me to be a strange process, but we turned some corner that day. Everybody copes in their own way, and while it wasn't a light bulb moment it was, somehow, a waypoint. My memories of my daughter slowly, very slowly, took on a happier note and up to recent years I pass her grave with a sense of fun; she and I talk. I don't believe Marian ever healed to the same extent. It was a taboo subject between a couple who talked about everything, and unless Marian specifically raised the subject, we only discussed happy memories of our daughter.

It is compulsory in certain countries in Europe that the children are brought to see Auschwitz, and a guide explains all the horrors that happened there. That day, I watched the children disembark from their bus all happy and joyous.

Did their joy stem from having a day off school? Or was this just another adventure in their eyes?

Over the years, we had gone to see the endless white crosses: Normandy, the Somme, the fields of Waterloo. I thought about the 20 million Russians who died in World War II, as I looked at these happy children, the innocent little faces now sombre, and could only imagine what was going on in their minds. I have to assume they thought this had happened long ago and, however horrible, that it wasn't in their time and they would know better. Since these death camps had become shrines to man's inhumanity, they have become monetised. You pay for your lunch, you pay for your Coke and you pay to get in. So it's just another peep show, part of a school outing – nothing to do with us.

Some years later, we went to Vietnam where around 500,000 young American men died, and God knows how many others were left mentally damaged, and I was amazed at how quickly humanity forgets savagery again and again. And we repeat it again and again. It is thought that five million Vietnamese died in their own country in this war, but nobody was counting.

Then we travelled on to Cambodia where we visited

the killing fields of Pol Pot, mound after mound of corpses stretch into the jungle, two or three million, nobody counting. I began to feel like the children on the bus. This was another horror story; a day out for us, another box ticked. It appeared to me that geography and race play an overactive part in our condemnation of genocide; the further away from us the atrocities are committed, the less concerned we are. I had learned nothing except a confirmation of humankind's indifference to the suffering of others.

We are currently fighting a war in Ukraine which gets high media profile because it's near us and it's newsworthy. As I write there are somewhere in the region of 50 bush wars in sub-Saharan Africa, but nobody reports on these in our media as a few million people are dying from bullets or starvation or both.

But this time, in 2002, this time we felt that maybe we could make a difference.

Despite the fact that Finucane and I had no idea what we were doing, we had experienced old hands who were prepared to hold ours. With the help of Brendan Rogers and the Department of Foreign Affairs, we started talking to aid workers and farmers, did some work with Médecins Sans Frontières and began to look closely at how this HIV/AIDS pandemic was ravaging Africa. And suddenly, somehow, we were in deep in projects that would keep us grounded in South Africa for 20 years.

One thing always led to another. Once you got involved in building foster homes, childcare facilities and schools, these led back or forward to even more basic needs, such as feeding schemes for orphans and child-headed households.

Back then 1,000 South Africans were dying every day from AIDS. So many children were dying in Khayelitsha that we had to buy a graveyard about half the size of a football pitch. The little white crosses that marked each grave marched into the distance like the crosses in war cemeteries. I remember very few of the children who lived, but by and large I remember those who died.

Government spokespeople routinely minimised the numbers who were dying and claimed they were coping. I think they took the view that a lot of people would die, and it would eventually burn itself out. From our experience on the ground, the only reliable figures were those documented at the beginning. In normal times, everybody was buried on a Saturday morning when the gravediggers were off work, and funeral attendances were as big as any Irish funeral. But at the height of the crisis, there were so many deaths that lonely funerals were being held on a Tuesday and a

Wednesday as well. That was just one indicator of the numbers that were dying.

Some Irish schools were taking an interest. We got a call from Eleanor Ryan, the mother of a Blackrock College boy who had just done his Leaving Cert, and she suggested we invite some of the students out to help with the building work. Instead of going on the customary post-exam holiday blowout, those boys were the first post-Leaving Cert class to join us in Africa. With them came their mothers and fathers and some serious funding. They helped to build another 10 orphan houses around Khayelitsha.

It was quite an education for them.

They were witnessing not just desperate poverty but also the extraordinary work of priests, religious orders of nuns, activists and organisations such as Médecins Sans Frontières (MSF), who worked with us on the ground and who were sometimes forced to smuggle vital anti-viral drugs into the country. It was MSF staff, with activists, trade unions and people dying from AIDS, who used mass protests and the courts to fight the profiteering big pharma companies for free treatment for all.

Then suddenly new antiretroviral drugs came on the market. The little white crosses stopped marching down the field.

It was MSF who encouraged Friends in Ireland into the next phase of its South African journey by inviting us to go with them to the Eastern Cape – home of the old tribal lands – and KwaZulu-Natal. To be honest, Marian and I were madly flattered that they would consult two total gombeens like us, so of course we said yes. In another piece of randomness, around the same time, we got a letter from someone who signed himself 'Liam' from a place called Kokstad in the Eastern Cape, saying there were 50,000 orphans there and he didn't know where to turn. He had heard we were helping orphans in Khayelitsha and asked if we would come and see him.

'Liam' turned out to be Liam Slattery, the bishop of the diocese of Kokstad and a remarkable Irish Franciscan, who spoke nine African dialects and subsequently became archbishop of Pretoria before retiring a few years ago after serving in South Africa for half a century. Even Marian – who deemed all men with a collar to be somewhat suspect – came to regard him as one of nature's great gentlemen.

The Eastern Cape was extremely remote, hauntingly beautiful, deeply tragic and more challenging than we could have imagined. We had been there a few years beforehand, and I vividly recall driving at sunrise through Umzimkhulu, the gateway to the tribal lands, with the Drakensberg mountains fading away into the sky. We both took it in, then said in unison, 'Cry, the beloved country.' We were not being particularly original, just echoing the title of Alan Paton's 1948 novel, which opens with some of the most beautiful lines in English literature, describing dawn over Umzimkhulu. 'There is a lovely road that runs from Ixopo into the hills. These hills are grass-covered and rolling, and they are lovely beyond any singing of it ...'

That morning, children ran along the road beside us, and their parents stood outside their rondavels, the typical round African huts, and waved. Despite huge backlogs in rural areas, there was some evidence that people's lives had been improved since democracy arrived in 1994.

By the time we returned a few years later, the plague had struck and death was staring us in the face. The men brought it home from the mines, and they died and died and died.

The signs were not encouraging. The scale of it was staggering. Most of the tribes had a deep hostility towards one another and were very fractious. Finucane, always more conservative than me in our decision-making, was very cautious about setting up in that remote place. 'You know we're only here for a look?' she'd say.

We spent a lot of time in discourse about it, as we did about many things. Her main worry was that we knew nothing about the area. We had been to Auschwitz, the Killing Fields and many terrible places, and our conversations always came back to the same point: somebody should have done something; somebody should have said stop. And this, surely, was our 'stop' moment?

We could say we were only foreigners here and, well, it's really not our business, and walk on. Or we could say, right, we'll do something. 'OK,' said Finucane, 'but we'd better set goals on this because it's crazy.' So, we shook hands on a pact – I think we may have kissed on it as well. If we saved one child's life, we would have done well. One child. Just one.

It was a reasonable target because we felt it wouldn't drive us completely insane. If we set out with the mission of solving the problems of the Eastern Cape – the poorest province in the country – or of KwaZulu Natal – the second poorest and said to be the epicentre of the global pandemic – we would run away because the extent of the poverty and deprivation made them insurmountable. Between them they made up about 40 per cent of the national population and it was estimated that nearly a quarter of the Eastern Cape had HIV/AIDS. In the five years since 2002, the number of orphans in South Africa had soared by 700,000. Many of the husbands and fathers had died from HIV/AIDS. Their widows, almost inevitably infected too, were transported down the mountains by wheelbarrow to where they were picked up by bus and dropped at the hospital to die. We were on the sharpest learning curve of our lives.

For Marian and I, all we could do was try our best to tackle each issue one by one. Nobody had an answer but at least we were coming up with half-baked solutions. It was a real roller coaster; all our emotions, and indeed those of the Africans, were on the table.

Tears, laughter, anger, sometimes a reward; it was a very powerful feeling when you knew a thousand children went home with their tummies full each night.

The reality was that the reward for us was wonderful. It seemed to me, and this was only an observation based on what we experienced at that time, that people who have nothing laugh a lot more than people with little. Perhaps they are closer to their emotions, but a meal in the day means lots of joy and laughter. A school room repaired, something as simple as putting in a window to keep out the rain, brought more joy and cause for celebration; everyone had to sing and dance for us to show their pleasure at such simple tasks.

A concept that is hard for us Westerners to understand is the concept of literally having nothing. We have so many fail-safe situations in Europe. If we knock at any door we could get a slice of bread, but here there was no bread behind any doors.

Some of our better plans for self-development didn't always work out as intended. I was in a settlement on the edge of Johannesburg where a nun was trying to help a series of family squatters who were now living on an abandoned firing range: children and adults were blown up from time to time from unexploded ordnance. The army had failed to clear up their rubbish. We asked the nun what would she like most to help the people and she said, 'Some hens'. A woman down the road was able to sell six eggs every day on the side of the road and keep her family alive. We agreed to buy a hundred hens (50 euro) and together we would start a chicken industry. About a year later, I returned to see how the poultry business was doing. There were no chickens to be seen. The kids had chased them across the firing range and every so often a hen would blow up in a puff of feathers. They had cleared a path to the old copper shell casings, which were far more valuable, and the adults sold those as scrap. At least it saved a lot of young limbs.

Music and laughter were spontaneous despite the misery that surrounded us.

One day, high up in the Drakensberg mountains, we were with a group of children and their parents from Portmarnock and had joined the local community for Mass. Mass lasts for about four hours. They had a band that played different sizes of Wavin pipes, I think they hummed into them, and they had one woman with a bell. They sang and they played their Wavin pipes in the most joyous way. At the start of the Mass, the young Franciscan priest gestured that I was to sit beside him at the altar and he said, 'The people want to make you King of this area for today.' Without further ado, they gave me a throne and a crown (a fabulous wicker creation that I am looking at here beside me now as I tell this story).

Finucane said I was the most embarrassingly red-faced king she had ever met and I couldn't disagree.

Halfway through the Mass, to my horror, two men led in a sheep on a halter. I immediately thought, 'I am not going to do this.' It was clear they wanted me to kill the sheep, which was obviously some kind of custom. I pointed to one of the mothers from Portmarnock and said, 'She'd be better able to do it than I, as she's a doctor!'

The would-be female executioner let one shriek out of her and ran out the door. The sheep was blessed and led out the same door. When I next saw him he was chopped in pieces cooking away on a tar barrel. The Mass continued in three different languages – Hosa, Pondo and English – while we waited for dinner (which I declined to eat).

Years later, I met the lady from Portmarnock and I said to her, 'You ducked your duties on the day.' She said, 'I couldn't kill anything, and secondly I'm *vegetarian*.'

*

Along the way, we were joined by remarkable people, many of them volunteers channelled through Comhlámh, funded by Irish Aid. Others came through Slí Eile and Magis Ireland. Vivienne Fenton found her own way to us. She was 28, earning mad money working in computers, systems control and project coordination with Wyatt and living the high life of the young Celtic Tiger when she began to perceive little purpose to it. She had seen the documentary on our work in Cape Town, and her curiosity had also been piqued by Niall Mellon's epic construction work in the townships. It all aligned with a wish to travel and a romance of some sort with a South African. One day in 2005 we had a meeting in the Poitín Stil in Rathcoole, and I told her I was flying to Namibia in a few weeks. She joined me on the flight. Her South African romance didn't last, but her relationship with South Africa endured for 10 years.

*

How do you help hungry, orphaned children? How do you develop community centres? How do you get antiretroviral drugs – if you can obtain them – out to a rural community with no infrastructure?

You give the children full tummies and keep them alive and hope the cavalry is just over the hill.

You develop a community. You learn that it entails a lot of energy and money, a reasonable amount of logic and a million per cent of emotion.

A lot of time was spent travelling on dirt roads to areas of fantastic remoteness. With hindsight, we realised we should have selected more populated areas. There were no signposts, no GPS. Liam Slattery used to draw maps for us which said things like turn right at the big tree or at the fence across the river – only there was probably no river because it was the middle of summer.

But we were usually following a nun anyway. The nuns were the main people in the area: they knew everybody; they knew who was in need. Sister Constancia, a tiny woman, carried a big walking stick that she used to warn off or even beat men who were battering their wives. The nuns had the community on their side. They used to walk miles every day, and when we got Sister Constancia a Mitsubishi Colt, she started to run the area like a mini-king because now she had transport. Jobs that used to take hours and hours, like dropping off food to remote places, could be done in a fraction of the time. If she heard some local villain was beating his wife, she could get to him faster. Nuns were the people to follow. I remember trips through wild storms, lightning and hailstones, and our only guide would be Sister Constancia or Sister Nathaliya driving ahead in a battered red jeep at 100 miles an hour. It was through Sister Nathaliya of the Daughters of the Charity of the Sacred Heart of Jesus – a powerful Black nun with a larger-than-life personality, introduced to us by Liam Slattery – that we met the extraordinary ladies of Nomlacu (Bizana) who were feeding orphans from a shed on the side of the road. This led to our first project in the Eastern Cape.

The nuns quickly got the hang of the computer skills that Vivienne taught them and learned to use the Vodafone card that slotted into a laptop. Soon they were trying to pick up signals way up in the mountains, communicating with us from thousands of miles away in the remotest parts of South Africa.

From my memories, the senior nuns seemed to be the only people trying to do something – and the principals of many of the schools. There were also great priests – probably denigrated as old white men, but people with great hearts who had stood up to say no during the apartheid times and got into a lot of trouble for it. Being men of the cloth, they had some sort of protection, of course. I really don't know how the religious sisters managed under those conditions.

At one point, the South African government was preaching to people to wear condoms because they were dying of AIDS, while the Catholic Church was saying, 'No, no, they're bad.' Of course, the nuns were in the middle saying, 'Hand them out, just hand them out.'

There were so many extraordinary, bright women, some of whom hadn't joined up for the obvious reasons. One 19-year-old told us she had become a nun as a protection from rape. The veil provided a degree of personal security, and she also knew that she would get some kind of education and escape from poverty. Friends in Ireland paid for a university education for her, and she now works with a well-known tech company.

The solution to one problem often led to a different

challenge. When they were available for children, the antiretrovirals, a miracle cocktail, were a complex prescription, which presented problems for grandmothers – it was always grandmothers – who were generally illiterate and unable to read the directions. So the children were dying and the parents were dying. It felt as if everybody was dying.

I recall being high up in the mountains with Marian, where women wore black cockade hats to indicate they were widows, and I asked about one such woman who was obviously very ill with AIDS. Sister Nathaliya told us the woman had five children of her own, and when her sister died of AIDS, she had taken in the sister's five children too. There was no support of any kind for a woman in that predicament.

I remember travelling across mountain tracks with Vivienne to pick up a four-year-old child who was suffering from AIDS. We found her living in a hut with no electricity, no running water, no transport, and caring for her granny who was dying and unable to get up from the floor.

We took both of them in a jeep down the mountain, an hour and a half on a dirt road, to the hospital in Matatiele. At the best of times, South Africa was an extremely dangerous place to drive, and most of us witnessed horrifying crashes. But Vivienne would do that gruelling journey again and again, get the child rehydrated and filled with nourishing food, knowing that it was only a matter of time before she died. In that world, it was always clear who was going to lose.

Marian said to me one day in despair that we were continually seeing the same children come back to us, starving or dying of AIDS or something else. Maybe they should have been allowed to die in dignity the first time, she thought.

We had come to the conclusion that we could only help the children. So we set up 10 centres where they could get a meal and be looked after to some degree. We organised classes, and when the Irish schoolchildren came over from places like Portmarnock Community College, they gave them lessons.

Portmarnock's trips were fostered and led by Niall FitzGerald, a teacher who was – and remains – very keen that students should expand their brains and their horizons. Its catchment area captured the spectrum of trades and professions. Plumbers, plasterers, carpenters, electricians, doctors, dentists, architects and more rowed in with their vital expertise, and between parents and students, over 100 Irish were landing in South Africa every year, with teams of key people going out every few months.

There were education teams, health teams and construction teams, so the students were exposed not only to every kind of reality but also to the magic of skills and teamwork. An important skills exchange was built into the programmes. Local men were superb plasterers, for example, and on both sides we had people who knew exactly what they were doing.

For teachers, Niall's education team introduced the concept of a child-friendly school. It worked because they didn't merely seek to eliminate corporal punishment but gave teachers the necessary classroom management skills.

It had an extraordinary effect on these children of the boom who suddenly felt the sharp slap of poverty in all they were witnessing.

We built health centres, feeding centres and orphan houses, which subsequently became crèches. In one area we built a complex named the Village of Hope, where children with HIV/AIDS from remote areas could be cared for over extended periods, kept warm, well-nourished and built up so that the antiretroviral drugs would work.

And in the course of all that, Irish teenagers learned what AIDS, sickness and death were like close-up and how families imploded. They also learned what it was like to be Black in a time when apartheid was still a very recent memory in people's minds. It was a live issue.

Relationships were critical to everything we did, and a completed project was always marked with a simple dinner, to which we invited all the key, essential people from the health and construction teams, the chieftainship and local government, all with a view to building on that essential trust. Sometimes caterers refused to serve us because there were Black people among us. On other occasions, white companies refused to hire out plant machinery to a 'Black' project.

At one stage, we were building a school high up a mountain, and we needed accommodation for around 150 people. There was a large caravan park nearby – but for whites only. I went to meet the owner and said I noted his caravan park was closed for the winter and offered to bring him a few hundred clients, who were here to do charity work, if he could do it for a reasonable price. He was delighted. So Portmarnock – and Sutton, Howth and so on – landed en masse and everything went smoothly until Sister Nathaliya came to join us for dinner one evening. Dinner was delayed, then delayed some more, to the point where Niall FitzGerald became curious because the volunteers had been working hard all day and were hungry. Finally, I went and asked when dinner would be served. 'When your friend leaves,' said the manager. No food, in other words, as long as Sister Nathaliya was on the premises. No Black person would be served, period.

'These people will be coming every year,' I said. 'You've just lost around 400,000 rand's worth of business because of your stupidity.'

He just turned his back and walked away.

The alternatives were limited. We next tried another place run by a white ex-officer of the South Africa police – usually a pretty brutal combination. I explained our predicament and asked if he had a problem. No, he said, he had once been a bounty hunter. The good news was that he didn't hunt Black people anymore. He made sure everyone had a great time and just vanished every night when Sister Nathaliya and some other Black people – mainly women – came in to tell the story of apartheid to our wide-eyed 17-year-olds.

The other side of that story, as seen by younger volunteers, was how judgemental we were about white South Africans then, around 10 years after apartheid. There was no excuse for them. Many were racist, openly and egregiously so. The difference between them and us, however, was that they were challenged almost every day about their racism, whereas in Ireland we rarely had to face up to our own inherent biases. Many white South Africans acknowledged their racism, acknowledged they grew up in that system and were indoctrinated by their church, went to segregated schools, never had to stand in line, always were told they were the best and given every opportunity. Then the poor young whites – relatively poor, at any rate – joined the army and at 18 were sent on patrol in townships like Khayelitsha with guns.

The consensus was that the younger generation definitely wanted to change, to be part of the new South Africa, and believed it was in their interest that everybody get on. But the older generations had a lot of work to do to shed all that, and some would never achieve it. It was simply a fact.

I suspect the students we sent back to Ireland had a more nuanced view of many issues.

Importantly, these students were also seeing signs of progress. In Kokstad, where we set up our headquarters, the legacy of apartheid was still evident in the contrast between life in the affluent town and the townships on either side. Then a white doctor bought a hotel in the middle of town and reopened it, and a lot of the better-off Black locals began to drink in the bar. The legacy of the Black curfew – a bell rung to order them off the streets by five o'clock – still lingered, so he provided an interior beer garden in case they felt uncomfortable on the streets. It seemed courageous, but he was looking ahead. 'This country was built for three million people and we have thirty-nine million now,' he said. 'I'm building it for the thirty-nine million.'

*

Working in the Eastern Cape presented huge cultural challenges. Children with albinism were in mortal danger from powerful witchdoctors who valued their body parts for 'magic' potions. When the witchdoctors failed to cure the 'bad spirits' of AIDS, they told the people that Médecins Sans Frontières had injected AIDS into them while the doctors were actually taking blood for testing. The result was that no one would take a blood test. Many of the tribal chiefs and officials were deeply corrupt, and we were warned not to bribe them, yet without their cooperation, nothing was possible.

I, for my sins, was appointed PR man for the witchdoctors. There were no other volunteers and I have to confess that, whilst they terrified the wits out of me, I soon discovered that if you stood back a bit from their bloody and fairly murderous careers, they also served an essential purpose in the tribal lands as resident physicians.

To give you an idea of their power: I was standing having a cigarette in a local market town one hot day, and in the distance I saw a group of people scattering. Coming down the middle of the street was a witchdoctor dressed in a long white skirt and his face painted white with a high cockade hat, holding in one hand in front of him the sacred bones.

People scattered so they weren't in his path.

When he got as far as me, he stopped and said, 'Hello, John, how are you?' I didn't recognise him under the paint and said, 'Do I know you?' and he said, 'Yeah, I was one of your first children.' He was referring to a food centre we had built!

I said to him, 'Well now, you seem to be our first graduate in the medical profession.'

He laughed. He was only a junior witchdoctor, but took great pride in his career path. I invited him to sit with me for a while and we discussed the serious work he was doing. It ended up with him giving me a pat on the back and saying, 'Anything I can do for you, if you feel sick or have any enemies, give me a call.'

He went happily on his way and I stayed smoking, much relieved.

*

I believe 2007 was when our collaboration with Bishop Liam Slattery and the buildings began to pay off. We were joined by volunteers Barney Shiels and Isabelle Fay and were beginning to establish a more permanent structure, with an emphasis on developing the capacity of community-based organisations on each programme site. Then another two Irish volunteers, Jennifer Aherne and Stephen Campion, arrived and we were starting to scale up, developing the capacity to help big groups while establishing systems.

Part of the challenge for Friends in Ireland at that point was trying to figure out its organisational structure. In Ireland it was registered as a charity, but it had to be established as a trust in South Africa in order to apply for government grants and other things. We were setting up memorandums of understanding with all these community groups and figuring out who we could work with. It was always about helping them to help themselves.

The magnificent women in Bizana and their enterprise stand out in my memory, women in sheds with pots trying to feed multitudes. Now they were women with proper facilities who were getting together a committee, organising rosters, feeding children and building gardens.

Sometime around 2010, when Maeve McKiernan, another of our young volunteers and life-force, was there, we completed a beautiful building for a feeding centre in KwaZulu-Natal. We found the right community workers, ensured they were happy and paid, and we had at least 50 kids going through there every day. They were getting breakfast before they went to school, then coming back for their after-school activities and homework.

It was up and running beautifully when the local tribal chief decided he wanted total control of it. That was a real shock. None of it had happened behind his back. He had agreed to the building, he was recorded signing the agreement, he was there in the photographs with Marian. But when it became successful, and therefore food was coming into the centre, he suddenly wanted to manage it.

I believe what infuriated him was that the local people managing it had their own bank account and, therefore, control of the money, and he had no access to it.

When men arrived with guns, we realised that someone was going to get shot. When we couldn't get agreement to a no-guns policy in the centre, we made the difficult decision to pull out our staff and leave.

*

Sometimes you won, sometimes you lost. I tried to play the role of diplomat, fending off the bribery and corruption parts, because the chiefs refused to speak to women – and that included Marian. Even Mandela had his work cut out in that regard. One of his toughest challenges was to bring the tribal chiefs on board, some of whom were paid puppets imposed by the apartheid government and, therefore, had a lot to lose. When the real chiefs returned to reclaim their positions, there was fierce resistance.

Apart from the fact that Finucane had a job to attend to, it was one of the reasons why I did a lot of the groundwork in Africa, travelling out there three or four times a year for weeks at a time. Marian had terms written into her contract that allowed her to travel there a few times a year.

It was exhausting and exhilarating and emotional. We never became desensitised to Africa over our 20 years there. We cried that morning driving into Umzimkhulu, and we cried when we buried children at lonely funerals. Yet those years were probably the most exciting time of our lives. A lot of issues were thrashed out around the kitchen table in Kildare. How do you get drugs up a mountain? How do you persuade children to come into the feeding centres? How do we protect children from abuse – where do they go? I believe we wrote more documents on child-protection policy in Africa than anybody else.

How do you persuade adolescent girls to stay in school

(you build toilets so they don't live in fear of snakes out in the long grass)? How do you stop the men carrying weapons into council meetings? What do you say to a tribal chief who demands a dowry in order to acquire – buy, actually – his fourth wife (the Irish government isn't giving any grants for fourth wives just now)?

While solving puzzles, we met some extraordinary human beings. A Franciscan priest from Athlone, County Westmeath, known as Father Bruno, had landed there by sheer serendipity in the 1950s. As young men, he and his *compadres* were en route to the China missions and, during a stop-off in South Africa, received a telegram telling them that China under Mao was no longer viable for missionaries and that they should stay put. Father Bruno made his way to Kokstad, and for 35 years he travelled around the mission on horseback, until he acquired a car. Each circuit took him six months, riding through the mountains alongside a mule that carried his vestments and the sacraments, while running secret literacy classes for Black adults and children. Marian was eager to record him and the stories, but it never seemed to work out.

He refused to say Mass in Kokstad cathedral for decades because it was a whites-only church until Liam Slattery's arrival. Even then, Father Bruno never changed. They gave him a parish out in the bush, where students from the Jesuits' Crescent College in Limerick helped us to build a school. Every winter he distributed blankets to families living in shacks in the swamp and around the dump.

Throughout our time in South Africa, we met men and women of faith who were deeply impressive human beings, and I speak as a near lifelong atheist. One of the most moving eulogies I ever heard was delivered by Liam Slattery at his mother's funeral in Tipperary, where he compared her newly liberated soul to untying a boat from a harbour wall, her spirit free to travel.

The schools that came out to work with us did not labour the spiritual dimension. I recall one institution in a very affluent area where we had high hopes of big donations. Marian and I went to meet the director, who praised all the wonderful work being done and so on before adding, 'Of course, there has to be a spiritual dimension to this.'

I looked at Finucane, who was staring at the wall, stony-faced. 'What exactly have you in mind?' I asked the director.

'Well, it's all very well feeding them and building them schools, but what about their souls?'

Finucane smiled icily and said, 'Our role is not to do anything with their souls – that is a personal matter between them and their parents and whoever their pastor may be.'

A polite argument ensued that ended with Marian saying, 'I don't think our operation will suit you because we're hands-on, really. The spiritual dimension is not within our ambit.'

Finucane's tolerance in that area was zero.

Generally speaking, teachers were actively seeking the benefits of the African experience for their students. It was a badge of honour for the young people to be out raising funds – they all raised their own money – to travel and work in Africa. Almost every student spoke of it as life-changing. Many had a huge spirit of social enterprise when they came back. Niall FitzGerald would say it opens up a new kind of partnership with parents, who were bringing their expertise and a cross-curricular approach right into the classroom.

It created a cohort of students who had a particular focus, who were exposed to a huge vista of life experiences, from job, to life, to living, to education, to health – it was all there. When they went for interviews, their African experience often became the focus because it was a sign of initiative, a sign that they had stepped outside the box.

For a lot of them, it influenced their career choices. Quite a number went on to study international relations. Some who are now grown into doctors, physiotherapists, planners and engineers continue to travel with Niall FitzGerald's team to work in Lesotho on some phenomenally advanced joint projects such as digital mapping, planning and development.

I'm well aware that some people, both in Ireland and Africa, are naturally suspicious of the white-messiah complex that often comes with this kind of work. We never saw ourselves as the great white chiefs – quite the reverse. I always linked somebody by the arm. Marian always deferred to local people – always. When they wanted her to talk, she would demur, asking someone else to tell the story if that was possible. In fact, I think our problem might have been that we weren't too well liked by the whites, but that never bothered us.

In fairness to the South African government, there was always a tricky balance between helping people and setting them up to make their own way in life independently.

That had to be respected.

*

Around sixteen years into our odyssey, we began to realise that we couldn't continue forever. The travel to remote places was becoming more difficult for both of us. There were concerns about my health, among other issues, and Brendan Rogers advised us to start planning our exit. That meant training up the people to run their own community centres. We employed a training charity, Starfish, to ensure that all the female leaders went on courses and were trained in how to apply for grants and access funds. It was always the women. Always. They were truly astonishing.

What was achieved? I think the most important thing is we managed to get the communities more organised to help themselves. We showed them there was money out there and that we couldn't get it but we could help them. And once they were organised, they were able to help more children.

What we did in a basic way was to feed some children, to ensure some children didn't die of hunger and to build some centres to help that effort. Liam Slattery estimated that Friends in Ireland helped some 20,000 to 25,000 children. We can never know for sure, but I know that, between us all, we made a small difference.

As Martin Luther King Jr put it, 'We all came in on different ships, but we are all on the same boat now.'

For Finucane and me, it was the privilege of our lives.

TEN

The End of the Ball

Cochin, December 2019

Finucane and I are sitting on a bench in Thiruvananthapuram in Kerala, India, holding hands, looking out across the Indian Ocean. It is a still, sunny evening and the sea is flat calm. The Angelus begins to ring. And then the bells are blending with the chant of the muezzin calling the Muslim faithful to prayer. The sound ripples across the water to us. 'They're playing your song,' says Finucane in that dry, amused tone.

I know.

I love the Angelus. I don't pray, I don't believe in God, but I like the Muslim call to prayer and I like the Angelus. It's a waypoint in my day, a 60-second nudge to stop what I'm doing when I hear it on the radio and press reset. Well, who am I? What am I doing? Where am I going? Is there a point to this?

I use the pause to reorientate myself into the now, an area I've always had great difficulty with. It always annoyed Finucane that I go along with all this despite being a non-believer, yet here we are. I find it useful.

We are coming towards the end of our holiday, and I embark on a kind of speech I've prepared. 'I seriously want to talk to you,' I say firmly (for once). 'I've been thinking about you and me for quite a while now in India. I want to say I am incredibly grateful to you that you were in lockstep with me during my alcoholism, and that you stayed through the worst of it. Now I want to return the compliment to you. I want to be in lockstep with you because you are now, like it or not, going for serious heart treatment. Because you and I have planned a great sunset walk, we have all the books in the world, we have all the time in the world, we have all the travel in the world ... You've just got to get better.'

She knows. Oh yes, she certainly knows. I've been carrying her for three weeks in India and can see she is falling apart. The cardioversion procedure she underwent shortly before the holiday clearly didn't work, although she never said so in so many words.

'You know and I know it hasn't worked,' I tell her. 'This has got to stop. No more of this nonsense – we're going to sort it. We're going to do our sunset walk – agreed?'

'Agreed.'

We buried her less than two weeks later.

I think about this at night. I think about the fact that I knew it was going to happen. Could I have done more? Could I have bullied her and said no, you're not going to ignore this? Why didn't I push it more? I think I know why. It goes back to our early days together, when we came out of our first marriages determined not to intrude on each other's private spaces.

A lot of people are carried into marriage on waves of emotion, impulses and needs not clearly defined. You have no idea how you will live with this person for 24 hours a day and how much of your character you have both concealed during your courtship. Are they getting the real you? Are you getting – really getting – the real them? Only time will tell. And then, if you're very lucky, like two old mill wheels you will slowly grind into a smoothness that melds you together forever. And sometimes that grinding through the mundane exposes a big mistake. Or you compromise.

In the early days of living together, we spent a lot of time *not* going back over our previous marriages because we had decided they had nothing to do with our union. As a strategy, it worked at important levels, but in doing so we were also establishing invisible distances from each other. Among our tacit understandings were the boundaries around each other's personal space.

Finucane, to a great extent, took that approach with me and my alcoholism – it's your problem, you solve it; if you choose this path, that's the path you choose. And in terms of her health, I knew for the last four years of our life that she was in mortal danger but felt unable to intrude on that vaunted privacy.

Sometime before the holiday, we had been in London and met our son, Jack, and his fiancée, Jenny, for dinner. Like all couples, we had meaningful looks and gestures for each other, a shorthand that is near incomprehensible to onlookers. Towards the end of the evening, Marian looked over at me and mouthed the words, 'I can't move.'

I turned to Jack and Jenny and said, 'Your mother and I are going out for a smoke when you two are gone, so we'll get you into the first taxi.'

While they were busy waving for cabs, I linked Marian out through the restaurant, then propped her against the wall outside, where I held her upright and lit a cigarette for her. With cigarettes in both our mouths, we probably looked more like old lovers having a smoke. I encouraged her to take a few deep breaths, assuring her we would soon be home. There was no point in directing the taxi to an emergency department. She wouldn't go. We performed that dance more often than I care to think about, and very few people ever noticed.

'We really have to do something,' I would say after each episode.

'Of course I will,' she would reply.

She was doing the most neglectful things with her heart. I knew that – she knew that too, I think. She tried spurts of self-improvement, and the conversation on her new regime could last for weeks – as she smoked through it. She smoked as much as I did, which was a lot. I always have a cigarette in my hand. I think I use them as a crutch, like worry beads – though, obviously, worry beads don't destroy your lungs. She had many stabs at giving them up and smoked the chemical version on occasion before reverting.

But there was this invisible line that neither of us crossed, one of the central lines that, in our understanding, made our marriage work. We worked terribly well at being together and independent at the same time. We were also very polite towards each other and were eternal optimists. We always believed something would turn up. It was a combination guaranteed to bite back. We both knew that Marian was on a steep gradient downwards, but deep inside we thought it would just go away, that if we tried our damnedest to ignore it then it wouldn't happen.

As in every facet of her life, Finucane was an incredibly private woman about her health. She didn't want anyone to know about her illness; she didn't even want to know herself. And she was deeply secretive about it. Looking back, we both had a barrage of medical consultations in 2018. She had COPD (as have I), but those consultations were mainly about her heart. After each visit, she would emerge with a 'Phew, no death sentence today … I'm fine.' I don't believe she was ever fine. She just ignored what she didn't want to hear.

She always had an unholy terror of doctors. I think she felt a sense of inevitability about her heart, due to her paternal side's history of early death. She knew the risks of very high statin dosages but reckoned they were a price worth paying if they kept her alive. At one stage, she sent her sister Dorothy to appointments in her place, and I suspect Dorothy did a better job of describing Finucane's condition than Finucane herself. The doctor would give his opinion, Dorothy would return with the news, and Finucane would say, 'Ah, that's grand.' For a highly intelligent woman, it was a serious blind spot. The charade finally wore thin on the consultant, who told Dorothy to send her sister in immediately and stop the nonsense.

So, though we planned the Indian trip as the holiday of a lifetime – reflected in the cost of it – it loomed on a cloud of anxiety. Everyone around her was anxious. India seemed an awfully long way away. If she got sick in Rajasthan, her Irish doctors would be in entirely different time zones.

None of these misgivings were coming from Finucane, though. She was just highly excited. Like Sinéad, who was too busy to cry about the wasp sting, Finucane was too busy to be sick. She loved her holidays and was passionate about India. We both followed the politics of the region, and she had a sense of unfinished business. I was sure it was the last big trip we would ever take, and I'm pretty sure she knew her long-haul days were over. Mind you, she was probably thinking the same about me after a bad run with a blood condition among other ailments. There was an air of anxiety over both of us, the big difference being that I showed up to appointments – after a hard poke in the ribs from Finucane, ironically.

*

At the same time, we were considering an interesting new era ahead. Her RTÉ contract was running out and, with some heavy encouragement from me, she was about to retire anyway. Her first grandchild, Jack and Jenny's baby, was due in a few months. We talked a lot about what our new life might look like in retirement.

We had started renovation work about a month before on our Dublin base – a little cottage beside the Dodder, a few hundred yards from the RTÉ campus – and were looking at a whole new way of doing our business.

But first she had to find a way of phasing herself out of a job and a schedule she had created and fostered to huge success. She truly loved doing her Saturday and Sunday programmes and loved being part of the national conversation.

She had fought hard for her success, and it was never as easy as it seemed on paper. The looming JNLR rankings of listenership figures were always a source of huge anxiety for her. The precarious nature of 'stardom' was laid bare in 2005 when she was ejected from her Radio 1 morning show – because her bosses were looking for 'fun and texting', as she often recalled in some distress and rage.

After that, in essence, there was nowhere to go if she wanted to work in RTÉ but the weekend graveyard slots, as they were then, and that looked a lot like a forced and humiliating retirement.

She did what Finucane always did. She gritted her teeth and did a lot of thinking and listening.

She listened to the advice of one prominent businessman in particular. If she was going to start something new on the weekends, he said, raise the bar for interviewees. Don't take the spokesman or the press officer: only go to the top. Go for the CEO, get the head of NTMA, get the head of the bank, and let it be known that they are the only people you will talk to and that you will give them a fair hearing. And that's what she did. When the crash came, her endless research, reading and knowledge of the main players – some of whom we knew socially – came into its own. She was even-handed, she knew the finance, she had read the bills, and she knew about banks. And they trusted her.

She and her producer, Anne Farrell, were a marriage made in heaven. They were quite savage in their criticism of themselves. At five past one on Sundays, after the show wrapped up, they went into an area of the garden in RTÉ and tore the programme apart – 'We should have given 10 more minutes here ...' 'He needed five more minutes there ...' 'We should have moved her first.'

My deal with Finucane was that I only listened to a

show if I was asked. I told her the last thing in the world she needed after a bad programme or after she and Anne had ripped themselves apart was for her to come home and hear me saying I'd been listening and it was a load of rubbish. They had tortured themselves enough, in my view. It allowed her to tell me what she thought of the programme without any comment from me.

Then now and again she'd ring me and say, 'I'd love you to listen to this.'

The one I balked at was an interview with Arthur Scargill. He had led the coal miners' strike in the 1980s and was at least partly responsible for the rise of Margaret Thatcher. I had no interest in hearing his paeans of self-praise.

But I listened. He was unrepentant, as expected. Marian, in her own mild way, said to him, 'You think it was a great success?'

He said, 'Yes, of course – we beat Maggie Thatcher.'

'Well, your membership plummeted during your tenure,' she said, quoting the figures. 'How do you consider that a success?'

He tried to bat his way through it, but it was obvious bullshit.

'What did you think of that?' she asked when she got home.

'Just confirmed what I always thought,' I said. 'He's a bullshitter.'

But Finucane had a macro point, as always. 'No woman should have to wait at a pit head for her husband or her son to come up,' she said, 'and I'm glad he and Maggie Thatcher killed the industry collectively.' That was her take. That's what she was aiming for.

Her all-time radio favourite was *Women Today* – probably because of its pioneering, crusading nature – but a close second was her Sunday show around the time of the financial crash. She knew what a privilege it was to get serious people round the table on a Sunday, people who knew politics, banking and whatever was chewing up the nation, and she loved the idea that she could have an influence on it.

When she got an interview with John le Carré – the last before his death – she thought she had died and gone to heaven.

How do you step away from all that?

As we edged towards her retirement, there were discussions about an online show titled *Men Today*, hosted by Finucane, involving her old RTÉ colleague from *Women Today*, Patrick Farrelly. Who else had the credibility to present a show like that?

Our grand plan was to live three days a week in Dublin and four in Kildare.

About a month before the Indian holiday, we were in bed watching terrible scenes on Al Jazeera from the Syrian war when she suddenly turned off the television, sat up and turned to me. Then without preamble or any notion of what prompted it, she said, 'You'll never know how much I love you.' Then she turned on the television again.

Her final broadcast – although we were not to know that – was on 8 December. Some listeners noticed that she sounded quite wheezy. They were right.

*

As always before any big trip, we had done copious reading and research and set off for India with the usual high hopes but with every intention of avoiding calamity this time.

We took the black train that runs all the way through Rajasthan, a kind of palace on wheels with gold-embossed carriages, thundering by night across deserts and by vast estates as we slept in our wonderful bedchamber, stopping by day near extraordinary Moghul palaces, forts and temples. We managed to have the fans kept running in our carriage so we could smoke as we travelled, and we dined alone together every evening on superb food, doing what we always did on holidays – talking, reading, talking ...

This mode of travel was chosen not simply for its various wonders but for the convenience. Marian could hardly walk at this stage. A taxi was needed if we wanted to move even a short distance from a railway stop. On occasion we moved around on elephants. A week before she died, I remember her sitting high on an elephant and remarking happily, 'Do you know, Sinéad would love this.'

'Yes, she certainly would,' I said.

As with any reference to Sinéad, the exchange ended abruptly.

The trip was planned around the five-day wedding of our friend's son, where Jack was to be best man. Sadly, our friend had become too ill to attend, which lent a deep poignancy to the rituals. I made a speech on his behalf, where I pointed out that Ireland was a small country but that when Mr Gandhi wanted a constitution, he asked our President de Valera if he could borrow ours. Both men, I noted, were particularly taken with the reference to 'freedom of religion' – upon which the low, droll voice of Finucane beside me murmured, 'That's stretching it a little.'

But we were romantics, Finucane and me. People sometimes compare wedding invitations to garda summonses, but for me, looking back, they crop up in memory in rich, moving variety. One of the most memorable days of our lives was the wedding of that fiercely determined young Japanese groom aboard a boat in heaving seas around the Galápagos. Finucane and I liked weddings so much that we got married not once but twice.

*

Our first wedding took place in New York in 1995. We told no one. It was five years into our life together, and it was a day infused, we fancied, with spicy flavours of Dorothy Parker, F. Scott Fitzgerald and the Jazz Age.

The bride and groom wore white – as you do – setting out hand in hand from Fitzpatrick's Hotel to walk to 1 Centre Street, Manhattan, otherwise known as City Hall. A few glasses were raised in a couple of bars before arriving at City Hall to join the queue of hope-filled humanity.

Marian was fascinated by the chat around us. She was particularly taken with the several versions of 'Do you like your new daddy?' drifting through the bridal parties.

Then it was our turn and, having said all the required words, the pleasant woman who officiated turned to me and said, 'You may kiss the bride' – to which we responded by giggling like schoolchildren. The officiant looked slightly taken aback. Realising we had to inject some solemnity into this situation, we duly kissed. Awkwardly.

Thus were John Patrick Clarke and Mary Catherine Marian Finucane united in matrimony for the first time.

Pleased with ourselves, we set out from there for the Oyster Bar in Grand Central Station where many of Fitzgerald's characters came and went and where we had champagne and an oyster for the sake of it, though we both disliked them. A big shout from two tables away turned out to belong to one of Marian's superiors from RTÉ.

'What are you doing over here?'

'Covering a story,' said Marian.

'Oh, you must come and join us.'

'No, we're having a think,' she said, which must have looked odd given our apparel and general demeanour.

We never objected to company, but this was to be our very private day. After an afternoon siesta, we went to the Russian Tea Room and later to the Algonquin, in homage to Dorothy Parker. As in all the best romances, there was a lot of laughter and a few tears.

That wedding was about fun, love and high adventure, but there was also a necessary legal underpinning to it. We were cohabiting in that Ireland where no divorce was allowed and separation was a hellish legal limbo, particularly for women, and the law had nothing to say about it.

From that angle, our New York marriage was about legal security of a kind. Marian's husband was still living. We needed to cross-insure one another for various purposes, including inheritance, property rights and large chunks of debt, in case one of us died suddenly. To achieve that we needed to be legally recognised in another jurisdiction where we could be married.

The big charade began with a trip to an office in Drumcondra where, on payment of a vast quantity of money, we obtained a divorce for us both – in Honduras. In Irish terms, it wasn't worth the paper it was written on, but for our New York marriage, those Honduran papers were all the evidence they needed that we were not entering a bigamous marriage. Our insurance company not only accepted it but suggested it – just one of the many bizarre compartments in the strange legal quagmire of Ireland Inc. which facilitated all those secret lives.

Twenty years later I married Finucane again, this time in Ireland, with less of the adventure and more legal formality and all the family in attendance.

Our divorce laws had changed by then, and cohabiting partners accrued rights in law. Catherine and I had obtained an Irish divorce and Marian's husband had died, so there were no legal obstacles to an Irish marriage. And our solicitor had made himself very clear. Unless we were legally married, there was a danger of leaving a litany of problems for our children. This marriage would be worth the paper it was written on.

Maybe that was why we were more wary of it. What did it say to our own romantic notions about ourselves? With myself at nearly 80 and Marian at 65, we had concerns, bizarrely, about interfering with the nature of our relationship. We talked about it endlessly. If for a moment we felt we were tied together by a piece of paper, it would feel terribly wrong, somehow. We had always felt as one. Now, we agitated, if we were to get married, would we take on roles that weren't really us – you wife, me husband ... that sort of nonsense.

The New York wedding had been pure joy, and we didn't have to think too hard about our relationship because we knew the marriage didn't apply in Ireland – come on, who's logical? – but the Irish wedding seemed more a legal formalisation of a wonderful 40 years, and we felt we just didn't need that.

Also, perhaps, our reluctance may have been something to do with the fact that a divorce was never as clear cut and as simple as some may tell you. For me there was always a residual guilt. I carried the sense of guilt silently for about twenty years. I didn't have the words or the will to deal with it. I had made a lifelong promise which was now in dust; giving my word was a serious business for me. One night in AA a member said to me, 'Whatever guilt you carry, forgive yourself.' It's a bizarre concept but, in my case, it worked and I was able to cope with myself thereafter. It's not just breaking your word, it's the combination of who you think you are. I have to imagine Marian was in the same boat, but it was a taboo subject that we never spoke of. I don't know how she coped!

There were practical steps in the early years. I only met the boys down the country. They lived in Dublin, two worlds. At their weddings we always used round tables for parity of esteem, so nobody was sidelined. We tried very hard to indicate to the children that whatever the differences were to the adults we were all working together so that nobody would be left out. I have no doubt that some of our differences filtered down to the children. They have very finely tuned antennas.

We had agreed that whatever differences the three of us

had as adults would never in any way be transmitted to the children; it wasn't their problem. Whatever thoughts they have in later life, they are now old enough to draw their own conclusions on the matter. Catherine raised three great sons, much credit to her; I always felt as part of my guilt that I got the easy part.

And Marian and I had lived our lives together because we wanted to, and we had long since learned that a piece of paper, one way or the other, didn't make for a happy union. We explained this at length to our nice, patient solicitor. After about five years of it, he ran out of patience. 'Cut the bullshit,' he said. 'I don't care what kind of love you have – just legalise it.'

'Why are you bothering?' people kept asking. That was mainly why.

Marian bought a lovely outfit and wore a hat for the occasion. We wanted to keep it very low-key but it leaked to the media somehow, and when we emerged from the registry office, a couple of reporters were standing outside. We were whisked away to Chapter One restaurant, where about twenty of us sat down, including Catherine's and my three older sons and Jack, along with Marian's sisters and a few mates like John and Patricia McCrossan, who had soldiered with us down the years through the good, the bad and the tragic. It was a great day in the end, filled with warmth, goodwill and laughter.

Looking back now, I realise that the gathering storm around Marian's health can't have been far away at that point. We never had the big conversation about death, not in any real sense. But we did talk about choosing our death. Incapacitation or dependency was not an option for either of us. We visited a solicitor to sign a living will in which we listed as many terrible conditions as we could think of where the other would be permitted to pull the plug and bring our misery to an end.

*

On the Monday we returned from India, the first day of the 2020 New Year, I mentioned that my son Neal was planning to come out to Kildare with his wife and children the following day. She replied that she was just very tired. That afternoon we were sitting around the table – smoking, of course – when she seemed so out of sorts that I suggested she go to bed. I told her I would sleep in the other room so as not to disturb her, and that Neal and I would meet in the city the next day.

Next morning, I went in to her with the usual cup of tea, and she seemed happily asleep with an arm thrown over the bedspread. I left the tea beside her and left. When I returned from Dublin in the afternoon, I looked in on her and realised with dawning dread that she hadn't moved an inch. The electric blanket was on, so she wasn't terribly cold.

Our road had finally run out. I suspect now she was already dead when I left her that morning.

A sort of numbness took over then. I sat there in that surreal situation thinking, *Finucane's dead ... But she can't be – only 24 hours ago we were sitting on a plane talking about women's education in Kerala.* I rang 999 and her sister Dorothy. The first responders confirmed that Marian was dead and kindly made me a cup of tea, but I sent them back to check again – 'You're wrong, she's not dead.' She almost made it to her 70th birthday the following month.

I wouldn't say I was 'able' to speak at her funeral because 'able' is not the word that comes to mind. I had to speak. I wrote something and read it back and thought, *This doesn't make one ounce of sense as to how I feel ...* And when I was in the church, I realised I had forgotten my glasses. It was probably a good thing. I got up and said what I thought.

I said that I wanted to talk about Marian, my Marian, a woman who I had loved for 40 years, a woman who for me always made the colours brighter, the world a bit easier to live in.

I talked about how excited we had been about the next act. We would have more time, more space, more books to read, more places to see; how we were like two 15-year-olds who were addicted to each other and who forgot to grow up.

The chief celebrant in St Brigid's Church in Kill that day was her first cousin Monsignor Ciaran O'Carroll, who had also officiated at Sinéad's funeral in Kilteel 30 years before. In his homily he talked about Marian's contribution to 'advancing and shaping our nation and its people through her professional work as a courageous broadcaster, and her determination to facilitate conversation without fear or favour was repeatedly and wonderfully captured in countless public tributes'. He spoke about her 'great empathy and sense of fairness', how she was a 'generous and determined woman, and a thoughtful and kind friend'.

We buried her beside Sinéad in the old graveyard in Kilteel as she'd wished. That evening, I felt I needed to talk to people who understood alcoholism and knew me well, so I went to an AA meeting.

I stopped obsessing about the causes behind Marian's death the day we got the coroner's report. It was found to be pneumonia – which was surprising enough for some to suggest we seek a second opinion. I never considered proceeding any further. My thoughts were that Marian was dead and it hardly mattered what she died from. It was a blessing, in a way, that she died in her sleep because she wouldn't have survived a stroke or incapacitation in terms of quality of life. She would have been the worst patient that God ever put on this earth.

It made little sense to rake over it all.

*

One of the first things I wanted to do after her death was to throw a party for her. I felt an urgent need to change things. There were pitfalls and disasters in our time together, but it had been a wonderful life. Then Covid-19 intruded.

My first proper realisation that she was gone from my life was when I turned to her to discuss progress on the old cottage on the Dodder, the place we designed together – she wasn't there, of course, and I realised I wasn't capable of making a decision on my own. We had had the back of it knocked down in November and planned to have it ready for our third act. As Marian used to say, if you want to make God laugh, tell him your plans.

I realised how much we chatted ... endlessly, idly, about nothing and everything. And how we read a lot together, companionably, in total silence. And how all those plans now lay in dust.

I remember realising all my touchstones were gone and I would have to reorientate myself like the old homing pigeon who flies round in circles until he finds the right direction.

The builder was a friend, fortunately, who kept the cottage project moving, and I was able to move into the old place that now stretches all the way back to a big, bright living area. Originally, I thought I would finish the renovation and then decide to dispose of it, but now I find myself happily spending time there, looking out the big window at foxes and birds padding around a Dublin 4 garden and thinking they're in the deepest countryside. Some days I head down the road for lunch in the RDS where my father spent most of his working life.

My other distraction is a Zen garden at the Kildare house, a project that may never end. The original plan has blossomed from a stream, a bridge and tea-house to three bridges, three tea-houses, a waterfall and a lake. It's where my mind goes when I wake up at 5 a.m. and is the diversion that carries me on into the day. I need practical things to keep me occupied, and a large part of this distraction is the unpredictability of it, not altogether sure what I'm doing or what I'm up against. At one point, part of the ground beside the lake shifted and two JCB diggers nearly vanished for a time.

At the beginning it was all about the vision, the execution and the cement and – not to be too grandiose about it – a legacy, perhaps, to leave behind me. I thought it would be too poignant a place to linger, that I would always be too sad to relax in it. I never imagined myself feeling Zen enough to actually sit in my Zen garden, yet here I am on a sunny morning in one of the little tea-rooms over the lake, with a pack of cigarettes and a coffee, watching the stream we constructed rushing downhill under Japanese bridges past hundreds of saplings, past tea-rooms and wayside figures, all the way down to the lake built with inlets channelled through bamboo pipes. I am surprised to find that it's one of my great pleasures.

And there are other things that I should be able to understand but cannot fathom at all. Before Marian left us, I happily talked to Sinéad every day as I drove past the graveyard. I asked her how she was, told her what I was doing and gave her bits of family and village news. It was a nice ritual. It grounded me a bit because my head could be anywhere. But now that Marian is there beside her, I can't bring myself to talk to either of them. Their togetherness has created some mysterious exclusion zone. I stopped saying hello to Sinéad. I stopped saying hello to both of them.

Of course, I remember being at the graveyard the day of Marian's funeral and thinking, *That's the end of this game, the game of being madly in love, the game of facing the world together. The game of the ups and downs, the emotional upsets, the interconnection between the pair of us*. And it was a great game. As her brother once said, we had a fatal attraction that caused a lot of upset, but Marian and I were also very good for each other. And suddenly, half of that unit is severed and you're thinking, *How does this work now?*

I know the physicality of a grave has deep meaning for many people, but it has absolutely none for me. I think of Marian every day, and I don't need a grave as a reminder of her presence in my life. I feel an odd discomfort at the thought of looking at a hole where two people I loved are buried. I've only been back once and need to go soon again, only because I can see the wall has been eroded by sheep and is falling down.

It's a beautiful graveyard, and it has all my history buried there in some way. But my history is also in here, in my head and my heart. In that sense I've moved on and I carry her with me, happily. This is the next phase; this is what we are going to do.

And whether I move on or not, the world has moved on. And today's excitements, like war, like Covid, like the simple fact of being alive, keep you moving on.

I carry wonderful memories of 40 years of a great companion, of bad times, good times, terrible times, skint times, sitting around this kitchen table and saying, 'What'll we do now?' I don't want to bury those memories. My moving on brings them with me. And it brings her spirit with me, and I talk to her quite a lot. Especially when I'm stuck for things, when my head just won't function the way I want it to, the way I suppose that upsets people.

There are limits to one poor body, and it's probably my age as well, but I've now grown accustomed to death, which I never was before. I now accept the inevitability and the randomness of dying. What choice do we have? Marian's two brothers, Tomás and Noel, died the same year as her. Three great Finucanes gone in a year. My only sibling, Elizabeth, died in 2021 at the good age of 87. Though we might not see each other for months at a time, we were very close in many ways, and the conversation would continue like it was only yesterday. She had cancer and had money enough to seek second and third opinions, but she was reconciled to death. 'I've run my course, that's it,' she said. I didn't argue. She came out of the mountains for Marian's funeral, which amazed me, well protected by her fine, grown children, and I was very happy to see her.

I was diagnosed with cancer in 2021 and it set off a whole new train of thought. It's a theme that I come back to again and again, about the randomness of life and death. We tried to leave a mark, hoping we did some good in Africa and planting a lot of trees in the daft hope of erasing our carbon footprint.

No one goes on forever and I have a litany of ailments. I've had 12 weeks of radiation for cancer on a lymph node. I don't make enough blood so need regular blood transfusions. I have COPD (while smoking like a train), I need stents, and my reading ability is curtailed by cataracts.

Yet I'm actually quite content within myself.

I race around a lot in the jeep with Bella the Kerry sheepdog, and I still have a lively interest in the horses. The Clarke boys are great fathers and great sons. I talk to all of them nearly every day.

Part of this third act of mine is my grandchildren. I took

the two oldest down the Shannon with me in the summer. No parents, was the rule. And I found them fascinating, very bright and funny, but what I find most extraordinary now is the relationships between fathers and children. They're 16-year-olds, very bright, very sharp, and really adore their fathers in a way that I, in my day, was too damned awkward to appreciate or articulate. I feel very lucky to be a part of all that, deserved or not.

Marian and I spent a lot of time discussing whether we really knew each other. I believe I was as close to her as it is possible to be. We shared the difficult times of being outcasts, runaways, the awkward ones; the terrible lows of Sinéad's death and routine lows like the jobs that didn't work, the businesses that went wrong. We talked endlessly and yet, we both agreed, how much of a person does anybody really know?

Did we talk enough about the important things – or maybe we didn't know how to talk about them? Or maybe we were asking questions for which there were no answers. I don't know. But I just felt when she died – this was my sense of her – that she was now free. What she thought and believed or didn't believe didn't matter any more. All the controls to protect her privacy – none of it mattered any more. That was over. And I'm sorry we never talked more about death and what it meant to both of us – because I think we tend to bundle up all our beliefs and disbeliefs about religion and everything else, and some of the good gets thrown out with the bad. In all our chatter, when it came down to that deep personal conflict, it was never a combination she wanted to discuss.

In some senses, I believe that she has been liberated from all her worries, her unanswered questions, the meaning she was forever seeking. Her spirit can sail on, truly free.

As for me, I may be following my father's footsteps, which would surprise no one more than him. In the 1970s Desmond bought a house outside Newport in County Mayo, where he lived with my mother, who was daft enough about him to go live in the country where he wanted to be, and gardened to his heart's content. One day in 1979, after securing his raspberries, he had a glass of whiskey and said he felt tired, went to bed and died. It was a lovely way to go.

Sometimes I sit here and think about love and realise I truly don't have the language for it. I honestly believe that we talk *around* love. I still couldn't tell you what it is. I don't believe there is a language that describes clearly how things like hormones and synapses spark into unison and remain – in my case – forever.

And when all the synapses cease, and all the connectivity between two people stops, the words we use – no matter how good we may be at words – only skirt round the loss. They skirt round the emptiness. If I was to talk about loss and grief and love, they would come out as platitudes, meaningless, because I can't articulate it. The endless conversations and chats are the product, the result of love. But they're not love. Love is a great, glittering ball, I think, and when it ends, it's as if somebody has turned off the power switch.

I know I miss it. I can understand anger. I can understand hate. I can understand all those feelings. But I cannot get around the fact that you walk up the steps of a building, as I did over 50 years ago, and somebody is standing there, and that's it.

That was it for Finucane and me.